Digital Culture & Society

Vol. 8, Issue 1/2022

Julia Ramírez-Blanco, Ramón Reichert,
Francesco Spampinato (eds.)
**Coding Covid-19:
The Rise of the App-Society**

The journal is edited by
Pablo Abend, Mathias Fuchs, Ramón Reichert,
and Karin Wenz

Editorial Board
Maria Bakardjeva, David Berry, Jean Burgess, Mark Coté, Colin Cremin, Sean Cubitt, Mark Deuze, José van Dijck, Delia Dumitrica, Astrid Ensslin, Sonia Fizek, Federica Frabetti, Orit Halpern, Irina Kaldrack, Denisa Kera, Lev Manovich, Janet H. Murray, Jussi Parikka, Lisa Parks, Dominic Pettman, Rita Raley, Richard Rogers, Julian Rohrhuber, Marie-Laure Ryan, Mirko Tobias Schäfer, Jens Schröter, Trebor Scholz, Tamar Sharon, Roberto Simanowski, Nathaniel Takcz, Geoffrey Winthrop-Young, Sally Wyatt

[transcript]

Indexed in EBSCOhost databases

Bibliographic information published by the Deutsche Nationalbibliothek
The Deutsche Nationalbibliothek lists this publication in the Deutsche Nationalbibliografie; detailed bibliographic data are available on the Internet at http://dnb.d-nb.de

© 2023 transcript Verlag, Bielefeld

All rights reserved. No part of this book may be reprinted or reproduced or utilized in any form or by any electronic, mechanical, or other means, now known or hereafter invented, including photocopying and recording, or in any information storage or retrieval system, without permission in writing from the publisher.

Cover concept: Kordula Röckenhaus, Bielefeld
Typeset: Mark-Sebastian Schneider, Bielefeld

ISSN: 2364-2114
eISSN: 2364-2122
Print-ISBN 978-3-8376-5903-0
PDF-ISBN 978-3-8394-5903-4

Content

Coding Covid-19
The Rise of the App-Society
*Julia Ramírez-Blanco, Ramón Reichert,
Francesco Spampinato (eds.)*   5

I The App-Economy

Authority, Sensory Power and the Appification of Biocitizenship
From Tracking the Pandemic to Vaccine Passports
Giota Alevizou and Eve Murchison   15

Pandemic Solutionism
The Power of Big Tech during the COVID-19 Crisis
Felix Maschewski, Anna-Verena Nosthoff   43

II Staging Science Policy: Storytelling in the Public

Introducing Science through Images
Visual Knowledge Communication on SARS and Covid-19
Christopher Frieß, Ramón Reichert   69

III Activism and Counter-Narratives

***The World Is Falling Apart;
But You're Still Coming to Work, Right?***
Remote Labour and Memes against Capitalism
at the Times of the COVID-19 Pandemic
Christina Tente   93

Installation Art in Virtual Reality
Charlotte Kent   117

Biographical Notes   141

Coding Covid-19
The Rise of the App-Society

*Julia Ramírez-Blanco, Ramón Reichert,
Francesco Spampinato (eds.)*

This special issue of *Digital Culture & Society* deals with the concept of *code* in relation to the Covid-19 crisis. *Code* is intended both as a computer-based language to program software or apps and as a functional and visual language for organising administrative processes, visualising information, performing behaviour control, and reinforcing shared imaginaries based on surveillance and dread. This issue departs from the idea that both forms of coding have become dramatically intertwined during the pandemic and are structuring a new way of being in and seeing reality. This volume explores the new forms of data-driven surveillance and representation of the pandemic evolution at the level of real-time epidemiology, sensor technologies, science policies, push media, and the heterogeneous counter-discourses that try to subvert them.

The App-Economy

Is it the adoption of apps, social software and messenger services that emerged during the Covid-19 pandemic changing societies in the long term? With its feedback technologies, digital infrastructures, and online environments, this new set of media not only supports the government and health authorities in dealing with the epidemic but also multiplies social control in peer-to-peer networks (Couch/Robinson/Komesaroff 2020). Social networking sites and their comment functions, hypertext systems, ranking, and voting processes ensure that our everyday life and behaviour have increasingly become the scene of mutual observation and an opportunity for data mining. The location-independent use in real-time transmission makes commercially managed apps a suitable tool for media self-guidance techniques in standby mode. Although the development we have described is not new, this volume raises the question of whether the acceleration induced by the pandemic will change computer-aided social systems and if so, in what way? (Keshet 2020).

In light of the health infosphere and quarantine policy of Covid-19, push media in particular play an increasingly important role today (Goggin 2020). This refers to media formats in the form of apps, advertising, subscriptions, or newsletters that are sent to users without them requesting the content themselves. Push content and its parameters cannot be changed by the recipients, i.e. recipients cannot change the content themselves, but rather select it in a menu if necessary. The information from the sender to the recipient of the message is unidirectional and the recipient often has no means of giving the sender direct feedback about the content sent.

Other aspects of changing government regulation and commercial commercialization of surveillance and control can be explored in this context. In this sense, this volume also aims to raise the question of how these digital environments change social structures and lifestyles.

In their article, "Authority, sensory power and the appification of bio citizenship: from tracking the pandemic to vaccine passports", Giota Alevizou and Eve Murchison explore the pivotal role played by track & trace apps and vaccine passports in enacting dynamics of biopower during the pandemic crisis. The authors argue that through these strategic measures, the governments of various countries – a case in point being that of the United Kingdom – exerted control over a population of sense-able beings, advocating their responsibility, on both an individual and a collective level, in exchange for personal data.

In their article titled "Pandemic Solutionism: The Power of Big Tech during the Covid-19 Crisis", Felix Maschewski and Anna-Verena Nosthoff examine the power strategies of big tech companies using the novel coronavirus disease (Covid-19) to strengthen their political, infrastructural and epistemic influence. In doing so, the two authors offer the first comprehensive overview of Big Tech's multi-faceted engagement in researching Covid-19 and they focus on five key areas that can be defined as the dominant areas of industrial biotechnology research: "(1) mapping of Covid-19, (2) exploration of Covid-19, (3) tracing of Covid-19 19, (4) Treatment of Covid-19 and (5) Management of Covid-19."

Bodies by Numbers

A decisive effect of the worldwide spread of the coronavirus is the transformation of digital lifestyle media into state-used recording, storage, and distribution media. In the words of Lewis: "The Covid-19 pandemic has spurred the use of digital technologies that are shaping people's lives and interaction with society. Policymakers around the world struggle to navigate uncharted territory while civil rights activists are alarmed by the 'new normal' under *bio-surveillance* and fear that apps built for one purpose might end up being used for others" (Lewis 2020: 11).

With the pandemic spread of the virus, the tectonics of digital power may have shifted the way forward (Dean/Hardeep 2020). Mobility tracking is regarded by health authorities and government officials as a reliable data basis for enforcing political decisions as legitimate (Guasti 2020). Seen in this way, digital media take over the empirical basis of political action. Engelman has thus noted: "Digital epidemiologists design projects that utilise data from active and passive monitoring devices (such as smartwatches and phones) and from any potential trace that people might leave through their online actions and interactions to infer, collect, and survey pathological information" (Engelmann 2020: 223).

The disciplinary techniques of state surveillance and punishment are migrating into all areas of digital communication and affect mobile media (geo-tracking), stop corona apps (monitoring), social media (blaming), and selfies (self-evidence). The Internet-based biosurveillance represents a new paradigm of *Covid-19 health governance*. While traditional approaches to health prognosis operated with data collected in the clinical diagnosis, Covid-19 biosurveillance uses the methods and infrastructures of *health informatics*.

That means, more precisely, that they use unstructured data from different web-based sources and targets using the collected and processed data and information about changes in health-related behaviour. The two main tasks of the Covid-19 biosurveillance are (1) the early detection of epidemic developments and (2) the implementation of strategies and measures of sustainable governance in the target areas of health promotion and health education. With the development of apps, application software for mobile devices such as smartphones (iPhone, Android, BlackBerry, Windows Phone) and tablet computers, the application culture of Covid-19 biosurveillance changed significantly since these apps are strongly influenced by the dynamics of bottom-up participation.

While the new iPhone used to be a trendy consumer item for unrestrained self-marketing, in Corona times it is more like a digital ankle cuff or a spy satellite. Digital connectivity based on smartphones and apps enables evidence-based politics today, virtually in real-time. For example, the evaluation of mobility data from telecommunications companies shows the statistical reaction to ordered curfews. Police, health authorities, and IT companies have set up access systems to personal data around the world to make collective movement patterns visible, to search for infected individuals individually, and to monitor quarantine regulations in private. The extent of civilian tracking is unprecedented.

Staging Science Policy: Storytelling in the Public

One of the main focuses of this special issue is the staging of scientific representation, specifically images of the virus as discursive, factual, or imaginary objects, as objects of research, and as sources of popular affection (Simko 2021). This follows the ways in which "[t]he Covid -19 crisis shows the potential of well-staged forms of alliance between science and policy" (Van Dooren/Noordegraaf 2020). Before this background, the pandemic is embedded in public communication strategies and scientific popularisation practises that are involved in the discursive and visual spread of the virus as a *collective symbol* (Link 1996) and a mandatory element of a *collective visual memory* (Vinitzky-Seroussi/ Maraschin 2021).

The visual representation of the virus is also at the centre of the microbiological discourses that are being conducted today about Covid-19. Against this background, we can analyze processes between scientific practice and the technical-medial and visual techniques of popularisation. (Vaughan-Lee 2021). In this context, both the representational and narrative styles and characteristics, as well as the historical references to the staging of objects of knowledge, can be examined. Using the example of selected representations of the virus, we here try to show how visual memory manifests itself in reception practises and how these visual representations distance themselves from their original reference object and are enriched by new contexts and manipulations. Investigating these processes of remediation, approval, and dissemination has enormous potential for uncovering the media construction of scientific knowledge.

Along with this, media technologies of data acquisition and processing and media that design knowledge in spaces of possibility move into the centre of knowledge production and social control in the field of health prevention and social epidemiology. In this sense, one can speak of a data-based and data-driven approach in health services research since the production of knowledge has become dependent on the availability of computer-technological infrastructures and the development of digital applications and methods.

In the era of big data, not only has the importance of social knowledge changed radically, but also that of scientific knowledge. Social media, mobile devices and technical assistance systems today function as gigantic data collectors and as relevant data sources for digital health care and Covid-19 pandemic management. From this point of view, digital media and their technical infrastructures always function as control environments and data-based surveillance tools, which have taken on a new role in the context of Covid-19, which requires closer examination.

In this context, our attention is focused on the critical reflection and revision of a computer-based epidemiology of the social that develops utopias of a new digital surveillance apparatus and attempts to colonise the reality of life in society. According to Engelmann: "Digital epidemiology is enabled by deep and digital phenotyping, the large-scale re-purposing of any data scraped from the digital exhaust of human behaviour and social interaction. This technological innovation needs critical examination, as it poses a significant epistemic shift to the production of pathological knowledge. Given the sweeping claims and the radical visions articulated in the field (...*we can*...) develop a tentative critique of what I call a fantasy of pathological omniscience; a vision of how data-driven engineering seeks to capture and resolve illness in the world, past, present, and future." (Engelmann 2022).

Christopher Frieß and Ramón Reichert examine in their submission "Introducing Science through Images. Visual knowledge communication on SARS and Covid-19" the aesthetics and science communication of biomedical visualizations of virus microscopy used by various national and international health authorities during public exposure and communication on Covid-19. Using the example of the virus depictions circulated by the US Center for Disease Control and Prevention (CDC), the two authors make it clear that scientific images are not neutral and objective, but are enriched with dramatizations and narrative styles, with popular readings to stimulate.

Infographics: Between Dread and the Loss of Empathy

With the phrase "pictorial turn", W.J.T. Mitchell has acknowledged a turning moment in recent history, from a text-driven to an image-based culture (Mitchell, 1994). Within our "culture galvanised by visual evidence and quantifiable solutions" (Easterling, 2021), infographics play an increasingly important role, as tools to which our understanding of otherwise complex phenomena is delegated. The origins of these approachable visual representations, aimed at informing clearly, go back to ancient civilizations, from cave painting to Egyptian hieroglyphs, from Middle Age illuminated manuscripts to graphical methods of statistics developed in the Modern Age. Today, infographics echo big data, they try to visualise "objectively" a reality that is more and more transfigured and dependent upon sets of information, whose large size is beyond our capabilities of navigation.

Since the pandemic outbreak, interactive world's maps updated hourly became instantly available online, informing users of the evolution of confirmed cases, reported deaths, and other information on the virus' spread. Infographics have become a crucial tool for documenting and communicating the evolution of the pandemic. These include bubble maps, line graphs, scrollable animations, hand-drawn charts, and pictorial configurations, some key examples being archived in the online platform COVIC http://covic-archive.org/. Kahn argues thus: "Several of these concepts have significantly shaped the language we use to describe how we measure, experience, and fight the disease" (Kahn, 2021). While speaking a universal language, these graphic representations highlight the incommensurability of such a dramatic global emergency, that is the impossibility of making sense of it through words.

By reporting the magnitude of the pandemic without any commentary, these dashboards and charts also produce a sense of dread that is felt in the present and projected onto the future. This is why some designers develop projects that underline how reducing human lives to mere codes elicits a loss of empathy. A case in point is a gradient of tiny abstract units that progressively becomes a solid black block, which occupied half of the front page of the February 21, 2021, Sunday edition of the New York Times, documenting the dramatic increase of deaths in the United States. This issue of *DC&S* also reflects on the growth of information design during the Covid 19 pandemic and the artistic responses to it, identifying case studies and discussing how these infographics, with their rhetoric of objectivity, impact our very perception of life and what it entails to live under perpetual threat.

Activism and Counter-Narratives

The Covid-19 crisis unleashed at a moment in which there was a strong climate movement and groups such as Black Lives Matter were at a peak of visibility and organisation (Mirzoeff in Ramírez-Blanco and Spampinato, 2023). However, with its lockdown periods, and limitations in the uses of public space, the pandemic has dramatically challenged many of activists' spatial practises, in a time where in-person actions have only been possible in a very restricted manner. The period has been marked by grassroots community organising for mutual aid in face of the illness and its consequences (Sitrin, 2020) which sometimes has been made illegal, or by riots that spread like a wildfire in Colombia, Spain, or the USA.

At the same time, immaterial initiatives born in unexpected sites and with unexpected tools also emerged, such as Gamestop, a campaign in which amateur investors bought stocks temporarily destabilising the market. The question of dismantling the master's home with the master's tools emerges once and again in a period that is putting to test the hacktivist technopolitical hypothesis. To what extent can the internet be used as a political weapon after the advent of platform capitalism (Srnicek, 2016)? Can we hack the code? While Nation-states and big corporations have taken advantage of the situation with an exponential increase in monitoring and data mining, social movements are in a moment of reconfiguration. Increasing confusion, for some years now anarchist communication guerrilla tactics (e.g. a.f.r.i.k.a. gruppe) are being increasingly used by the so-called alt-right. Fake news and far-fetched theories have taken centre stage in pandemic times, and it has also become convenient for governments to discredit any criticism by situating it in this realm. In this space of ambiguity, conspiracy narratives develop as a form of folklore and myth-making that attempts to make sense of the complexity of a situation that seems impossible to grasp.

In this landscape of turmoil, working from within and without activism, this volume aims to reflect on how to think of post-pandemic social movements – and the relationship between virtual and non-virtual presence – in an ever more digitalized world. This includes the uncomfortable and complex relationship of activism with conspiracy theories, and the role of digital media in their narratives and dissemination.

In her article *"The world is falling apart; but you're still coming to work, right? Remote labour and memes against capitalism at the times of the Covid Pandemic"* Christina Tente examines the political undercurrents of internet humour during pandemic times. Analyzing photo-based Internet memes about remote labour, isolation, *zoomification* and exploitation, and departing from Stuart Hall´s analytical model she classifies and clarifies this myriad of images where laughter is the medium for anticapitalist discourses.

Locked down in their own apartments, several visual artists have explored the possibilities of emancipation offered by digital and immersive technologies, in line with a renewed idea of the virtual as the new everyday. Charlotte Kent in "Installation Art in Virtual Reality" discusses artworks developed on VR platforms by Carla Gannis, Kurt Hentschlagger and Matthew Gantt (in collaboration with Claudia Hart) during the first year of the Covid-19 pandemic, highlighting the phygical potential of installation art, in line with the earliest enthusiastic discourses on the metaverse. Humour and creativity might be two possible lines of flight in the times of Coding Covid.

References

a.f.r.i.k.a. gruppe, Luther Blissett, Sonja Brünzels, *Handbuch der Kommunikationsguerilla*. Berlin: Assoziation, 1997.
Couch, Danielle L., Priscilla Robinson, and Paul A. Komesaroff, "COVID-19—extending surveillance and the panopticon." *Journal of Bioethical Inquiry* 17/4 (2020): pp. 809-814.
Dean F. Sittig/Singh Hardeep, "COVID-19 and the need for a national health information technology infrastructure." *Jama* 323/23 (2020): pp. 2373–2374.
Easterling, Keller, *Medium Design: Knowing How to Work on the World*. London and New York: Verso 2021.
Engelmann, Lukas, "Digital epidemiology, deep phenotyping and the enduring fantasy of pathological omniscience." *Big Data & Society* 9/1 (2022): pp. 223–254.
Goggin, Gerard, "<? covid19?> COVID-19 apps in Singapore and Australia: reimagining healthy nations with digital technology." *Media International Australia* 177.1 (2020): pp. 61–75.
Guasti, Petra, "The impact of the Covid-19 pandemic in Central and Eastern Europe: The rise of autocracy and democratic resilience." *Democratic Theory* 7/2 (2020): pp. 47–60.
Han, Byung-Chul, *Psychopolitics: Neoliberalism and New Technologies of Power*. London and New York: Verso, 2017.
Han, Byung-Chul, "COVID-19 has reduced us to a 'society of survival.'" *EFE*, May 25, 2020.
Davis, Mike, *The Monster Enters: COVID-19, Asian Flu, and the Plagues of Capitalism*. London and New York: Verso, 2022.
Kahn, Paul, "The pandemic that launched a thousand visualisations." *Eye*, No. 101, Vol. 26, 2021. Available at https://www.eyemagazine.com/feature/article/the-pandemic-that-launched-a-thousand-visualisations
Keidl, Philipp Dominik, Laliv Melamed, Vinzenz Hedeger, Antonio Somaini, *Pandemic Media: Preliminary Notes Toward an Inventory*. Lüneburg: Meson Press, 2020. Available in OA at https://meson.press/wp-content/uploads/2021/01/9783957960092_Pandemic_Media.pdf

Keshet, Yael, "Fear of panoptic surveillance: using digital technology to control the COVID-19 epidemic." *Israel Journal of Health Policy Research* 9.1 (2020): pp. 1–8.

Lewis, Dev, "The bio-surveillance state: an emerging new normal in Asia." Heinrich Böll Stiftung (2020). Available in OA at https://us.boell.org/en/2020/05/08/bio-surveillance-state-emerging-new-normal-asia

Link, Jürgen, *Versuch über den Normalismus. Wie Normalität produziert wird.* Opladen: Leske + Budrich, 1997.

Mitchell, W.J.T., *Picture Theory: Essays on Verbal and Visual Representation.* Chicago and London: The University of Chicago Press, 1994.

Mirzoeff, Nicholas, *How To See the World.* London: Penguin, 2015.

Mirzoeff, Nicholas, *The Appearance of Black Lives Matter.* New York: [NAME] Publications, 2017. Available in OA at https://namepublications.org/item/2017/the-appearance-of-black-lives-matter/

Preciado, Paul B. *Dysphoria Mundi.* Madrid: Anagrama, 2022.

Ramírez-Blanco, Julia and Francesco Spampinato (eds.), *The Pandemic Visual Regime: Visuality and Performativity in the COVID-19 Crisis.* Galeta, CA: punctum books, 2023.

Simko, Christina, "Mourning and Memory in the Age of COVID-19." *Sociologica* 15/1 (2021): pp. 109–124.

Sitrin, Marina & Colectiva Sembrar (eds.), *Pandemic Solidarity: Mutual Aid During the Covid-19 Crisis,* London: Pluto Press, 2020.

Spiegelhalter, David and Masters, Anthony, *Covid by Numbers: Making Sense of the Pandemic With Data.* London: Penguin, 2021.

Srnicek, Nick, *Platform Capitalism.* London: Polity Press, 2016.

Van Dooren, Wouter, and Mirko Noordegraaf, "Staging science: Authoritativeness and fragility of models and measurement in the COVID-19 crisis." *Public Administration Review* 80.4 (2020): 610–615.

Vaughan-Lee, Cleary, "Student Voice: Photography, COVID-19, and our collective memory." *Childhood Education* 97/1 (2021): pp. 26–35.

Vinitzky-Seroussi, Vered, and Mathias J. Maraschin, "Between remembrance and knowledge: The Spanish Flu, COVID-19, and the two poles of collective memory." *Memory Studies* 14/6 (2021): pp. 1475–1488.

Žižek, Slavoj, *Pandemic!: COVID-19 Shakes the World.* Cambridge: Polity, 2020.

The App-Economy

Authority, Sensory Power and the Appification of Biocitizenship
From Tracking the Pandemic to Vaccine Passports

Giota Alevizou and Eve Murchison

Abstract

This paper examines how authority and governmentality were enacted through digital technologies during the COVID-19 pandemic. Through the proliferation of track and trace apps, as well as digital vaccine passports, the contemporary 'biocitizen' became someone who was at once participatory and sacrificial for the 'greater good'. Advancing a notion of sensory power (Isin and Ruppert, 2020) and app-enabled 'biopolitical authority' as a novel form of governmentality, this paper explores how the tracking and monitoring of individual bodies renders them 'sense-able beings' through the devices, apps, and platforms that they engage with. Drawing on a discourse-oriented analysis of UK-based government visuals and news reports surrounding the promotion (and controversies) of tracking apps and vaccine passports, we demonstrate that partaking in society as a 'good' biocitizen meant allowing COVID-19 technologies to pre-empt and influence bodily movements on both a micro and macro scale. As such we argue that COVID-19 technologies, ranging from tracking apps to vaccine passports, became 'pre-emptive' technologies that codified human bodies and their infectious status through alerts and notifications, which in turn, validated and reified a sense of belonging as a good and healthy 'biocitizen'. This paper will unpack these themes to propose ways in which sensory power was deployed to organise and structure societies, first at a responsibilised individual level, and then as a societal collective, throughout the pandemic. In doing so, this paper seeks to address the varying forms of control that came out of the pandemic, as well as the social implications that they then had on biocitizenship and belonging.

Keywords

Covid-19 pandemic, track and trace apps, biopolitics, biocitizenship, vaccine passport

Introduction

In this paper, we discuss responsibilisation and its relationship to the UK's contact tracing app, COVID-19 passes, and by extension, COVID-19 passports; as well the impact that these technologies can have on notions surrounding the contemporary 'biocitizen'. We propose that these technologies exerted 'sensory power' (Isin and Ruppert, 2020, p.1–2) over individuals as they were quite literally made 'sense-able' beings through the various forms of digitised data that they generated via clicks, check-ins, shares, notifications and saves. Such 'sensory assemblages' then became entrenched in novel 'intermediary clusters of relations' (ibid, p.7), which this paper will explore.

We propose a broad definition of responsibilisation as the displacement of 'responsibility' from the state onto citizens to enact a particular form of governmentality (Raitakari and Hall, 2017). This process of displacement occurs not through coercion, but through an 'appeal of freedoms' mechanism by those in power (Pyysiäinen et al, 2017, p.217). Within the context of the pandemic, individuals were primed to become the sole drivers of their health through the encouragement of self management and regulation (i.e self-tracking, self-isolating, digital passes, passports, and vaccination), in return for particular freedoms (i.e social acceptance and greater mobility), whilst questions of state responsibility including adequate healthcare, PPE and financial support became less scrutinised. In so doing, responsibilisation was indirectly enforced via a mode of 'subjectification' that endorsed self-governance under a guise of enterprising self-care (Rose, 1992; Peters, 2001; Barnett et al., 2008; Pyysiäinen et al., 2017). In other words, responsibilisation was utilised by those in power during the pandemic to enact a unique form of neoliberal governance that framed individuals as the sole drivers of one's [mis]fortunes within society. In this paper, particular attention will be given to *how* responsibility is framed discursively, and the consequences that this can have on contemporary conceptions of belonging, the subject and consequently, biocitizenship. Through an exploration of sensory power in relation to COVID-19 technologies, we first intend to show the various mechanisms, tools and agencies utilised to enforce this notion of neoliberal responsibilisation by those in power. We will then discuss how sensory power interlaces with symbolic and media power as those in power seek consent, command means of communication, and set agendas about modes of traceability. We thereby suggest that the interlacing of such power(s) have framed the struggles, tensions and contradictions that have defined some vocabularies in public debates.

The COVID-19 pandemic was the first to occur against a sophisticated global digital backdrop in public health management. Therefore, digital responses in the form of contact tracing apps, data dashboards, AI, digital thermometers, wearable technologies, machine learning, telemedicine and global positioning systems were all deployed across the globe to 'facilitate pandemic strategies and responses in ways that are difficult to achieve manually' (Whitelaw et al, 2020, p. 435).

Aiming to contribute to burgeoning research into the social impact of emergent digital technologies within public health, this paper focuses on some of the ways in which apps enacted governance and authority over individuals, communicated through a rhetoric of responsibilisation. As such, we conceptualise COVID-19 modulating apps as technological assemblages (Kitchin, 2014), inter-facing an embodied traceability (track and trace) that order, arrange or objectify a verifiable right to mobility (e.g. the NHS covid-19 pass which has, by extension, been coined a 'vaccine passport'). We thereby question the 'mechanical objectivity' (Porter, 1995, p.215) of these technologies and seek to tease out the interrelationality between the social and communicative, design and implementation of contact tracing apps and appified vaccine passports, as well as the power and authority that they can enact.

As the COVID-19 pandemic was the first to occur within an age of digital communication ubiquity and growth, responses across the globe to track the virus were therefore primarily digital. In the United States the 'NOVID' app was adopted, whilst in Austria the 'stopp Corona' app was introduced, and in the United Kingdom the government implemented the 'NHS Test and Trace' app, all in an attempt to surveil the viruses' movements, determine 'hotspots' and contain 'epicentres' (Du, L, Raposo, VL and Wang M, 2020). As governments increasingly turned to technology to mitigate transmission rates, tech giants like Apple and Google were at the forefront. The duo designed an application programming interface (API) that conducted contact tracing through mobile phones and 'exposure notifications'; providing a foundational model that others could use to create COVID-19 tracking apps (Leith and Farrell, 2021). The pandemic thereby fuelled collaboration between governments, biomedical companies, and tech giants like Apple and Google, to hold unprecedented levels of power to a global health crisis (Kelion, 2021). The normalisation of public-private partnerships then not only created the conditions necessary for the near fetishization of technological, platform, and app 'efficiency', but also facilitated the normalisation of new forms of biopolitical authority in the name of open protocols and collaboration. This in turn legitimised mass surveillance mechanisms, which calls into question means of privacy and transparency, consensus and accountability. We therefore argue that the near fetishisation of COVID-19 technologies warrants a more nuanced understanding of the interfaces mediating between human/data relations.

Problematising the interfacial aspects of human/data relations may indeed be useful for revealing the conditions that underlie the framing of 'public awareness' (Georgiou and Titley; 2022). This can in turn lead to enhanced possibilities of concerted political action for the management of the pandemic; a political action that would be deemed productive if it were to create or constrict the engagement of 'responsibilised appified subjects'. Here, consent and voluntariness of the neoliberal subject who evidences 'self care' through isolation and 'bubbles', was framed around the invitation to establish a responsible 'us' as means of a commons; capitalised via concerted tracking and tracing, codified QR codes, check ins and 'pings'. This sort of encoded collective action brought about by capitalised tracking, not only involved varying degrees of self reporting, tracing, sensing, tracking and certification by some, but also conditions of exclusion, precarity and difficulty for others.

In their capacity to benefit some and not others within society, track and trace apps and vaccine passports facilitated inclusion and exclusion of citizens through binaries of protection and defence (Ajana, 2013, p.52). Thus 'citizenship' is an apt metaphor to explore who benefitted from such technologies and who was further disadvantaged. By extension, 'biocitizenship' considers belonging and societal inclusion/exclusion through aspects of the biological. That is, technologies such as the UK's track and trace app and vaccine passports sort through 'forms of life according to their degree of utility and legitimacy in relation to the market economy' (Ajana, 2012, p.851).

This paper proceeds with a theoretical discussion of sensory power and its intersection with biopolitical authority, continuing with a useful framework that we propose operationalises these intersections and exposes the mediating interfaces of human/data relations. We acknowledge that data visualisations and diagrams (e.g. curves and simulations) have played a key role in the visual culture of the contagion not only in describing, but also in predicting and advising on the types of controlled actions during the pandemic. Such visualisations, as Sampson and Parrika (2021) argue, reveal epistemic and aesthetic occurrences pertaining to a variety of policy making directions and responses. Our focus here however is on the representational order of pandemic technologies, formed as part of the *outcome* of such responses. Deploying discourse analysis to decode norms of visual semiosis using a small sample of pandemic 'interfaces', exemplified in promotional imagery of track and trace apps and vaccine passports, section two operationalises the relationship between biopolitcal authority and sensory power through three loci/themes that each manifest the tensions we seek to demonstrate: a) tech fetishization, b) capitalised tracking, and c) biocitizenship. Our discussion on each theme is further contextualised by relevant research, reviewing public perceptions and debates on pandemic technologies to highlight significant pairs of tensions on each theme.

1. Sensory Power and the Materiality of Aesthetic Assemblages

Central to our argument is how sensory power was exerted over individuals and in turn, societies at large, to create 'clusters' of relations (Isin and Ruppert, 2020, p.7). Whilst sovereign, regulatory and disciplinary power has historically sought to group individuals into categories of race, class and gender, sensory power seeks to group people together through *relationality* (Isin and Ruppert, 2020, p.8). In other words, engaging with track and trace apps and vaccine passports generated data over one's 'contact' with another either infectious or healthy person, which in turn became the object of interest for governments (ibid). Sensory power is therefore less concerned with the data itself, but with 'forms of power that produce and act upon it' (Isin and Ruppert, 2020, p.1). Sensory power thrives on relationality, and it is the relationality of beings, devices and coronavirus which led to the creation of 'clusters' (Isin and Ruppert, 2020, p.8). As individuals engaged with track and trace apps and vaccine passports daily to generate data, 'clusters' of the sick and healthy came into being. Here, clustering not only refers to the physical body per se, but also to the ever changing relations and sensory assemblages between healthy and infectious bodies through live tracking.

We therefore argue that such *live* tracking, particularly in the case of vaccine passports that have prevailed over track and trace since early 2022, cross boundaries and borders of locality, state and circumstance. Sensory power thereby operates differently to other forms of power in that it does not impose categories on society in advance, but instead brings clusters into being as a 'consequence of analytics such as machine learning and algorithms' (Isin and Ruppert, 2020, p.9). Authority is then enacted over clusters under the guise of individual responsibility and self-governance, as one's actions and movements became increasingly monitored during the pandemic and viewed in relation to others.

This relationship between sensory power and technology has become increasingly substantiated in the twenty-first century through various mechanisms including algorithms and big data (Noble, 2018), biometric systems (Ajana, 2010, 2012, 2013, 2017; Kloppenburg and Van der Ploeg, 2018), digital surveillance (McGregor, 2001; Brown and Baker, 2003; Davies, 2021), data colonialism (Couldry and Mejias, 2018) and self quantification (Till, 2014; Ajana, 2017, 2020; Gilmore, 2021). Crucially then, scholars in science and technology studies, postphenomenology, and media studies have argued that it is impossible to grasp the workings of datafication in health if one considers only larger power dynamics or the subjective experiences of data-generating individuals. As Ruckenstein & Schüll argue, one must also take into account the nonhuman elements that mediate between these dynamics and experiences, such as device parameters and affordances, as well as the processes and practices that surround them (Ruckenstein & Schüll, 2017, p. 268).

For example, sensory ethnographers Pink and Fors, have observed that the 'digital materiality' of self-tracking technologies intimately mediates 'people's tacit ways of being in the world' (Pink and Fors, 2017, p. 2). In their *mediating* capacity these elements may act with a kind of 'agency', 'liveliness' (Lupton, 2016, p. 114), or 'performativity' (Kitchin, 2014), that shape possibilities for action (Williamson, 2015, p. 141), thereby guiding, and thus, formatting or altering the course of a given tracked phenomenon according to their own classificatory and procedural logics (Ruckenstein & Schüll, 2017, p. 268). In other words, such apparatuses' and assemblages entail special materialities that inscribe specific behavioural responses or indeed produce certain behavioural outcomes. This in turn produces clusters involving a relationality between human and non-human actors, ultimately animating the interfacial complexes that manifest intersections of commercial, tech, state power and agency. As sensory-based technologies and interfaces rapidly evolve and play an increasing part in mediating our digital lives, it is important to critically understand both the *discursive* and *material* backdrop to their design and function.

Our conceptual framework is anchored around the ways in which sensory power creates new modes of authority and novel regimes of knowledge manifested in novel clusters of responsibility and self-governance. Extending our discussion on sensory power above, we illustrate that apps, devices and platforms are more than sources of data relations as data relations are also embedded in particular strategic narratives or communicative frames that appeal to (and manage) particular forms of behaviour. As such, COVID-19 technologies are a part of framing dominant perceptions of, as well as debates on, pandemic management. This may help in understanding how novel norms and regimes of authority among stakeholders are produced and enacted upon by those who consent or resist such powers. We therefore argue that new sensory materialities and rationalities of biopolitics, as well as the new assemblages and technologies of knowledge that they have produced, lend themselves to a need for a clearer understanding on how impressions and interfaces are encoded as discourse. This involves understanding how new biosensory or biosanitary norms may be internalised (or resisted upon) in visual/promotional material, and in public debates on what constitutes responsible biocitizenship. We begin unpacking these notions by discussing how novel aesthetics and interfaces of biopolitical authority may be considered a mediator between sensory power and responsibilisation, and how this also manifests at the core of data-human mediations (Ruckenstein & Schüll, 2017, p. 268). We finally discuss how this conceptualisation lends itself to a discourse analytical approach that charts our three cases: tech fetishisation, capitalised tracking and biocitizenship, alongside exploration of the discoursal materiality of data-human mediations.

1.1 Authority: What Does It Mean to Be Biopolitically Authoritative in Data Human Mediations?

Sociologist Claire Blencow (2013), offers a nuanced conceptualisation of biopolitical authority as a means to inform diverse strategies of empowerment, politicisation and authority-production. Seeking to address whether biopolitical relations destroy or foster capacities for politics, she offers a notion of plural authority that is often neglected in debates of power or liberal economic theories of exchange. More specifically, she considers 'authority as a type of power that works through degrees of openness, answerability, and trust between participants in authoritative power relations' (Blencow, 2013, p.9). This notion of authority is centred 'upon practices and structures of knowledge', and powers of knowledge that possess a role in the production of sharedness, boundedness and meaningfulness variously called 'community', 'sociality', and 'the common' (ibid, p. 10). Drawing on Foucault's work on biopolitics and governmentality (Foucault, 1980; 2003, Lemke, 2001), Blencow aimed to propose that politics could be instigated not simply through breaking given aesthetic orders (dissensus), but also through new aesthetic productions of objectivity (ibid, p.10). However, this production of objectivity crucially depends upon an understanding of different discursive frames and aesthetics of data-human mediations.

Communitarian aspects of Web 2.0 spaces, such as networked sociality, openness, transparency, public access and commons based peer production (Benkler, 2006), offer conditions that enable cooperation and a sharing of resources with the political 'goal' of coming together (as a community) for 'public good'. This has been variously used within a number of fields ranging from alternative media (Castells, 2009), information and education projects (Alevizou, 2017), to grassroots urbanism (Alevizou, 2021), and social movements (Castells, 2009; 2012). Notions of communication and power, proposed by the likes of Castells deploys a techno-dialectical analysis that avoids determinism, to offer compelling examples whereby the plurality of authority gives way to new aesthetic productions of objectivity surrounding political engagement, solidarity and collective action. Technological solutionism (Morozov, 2013), for example, has spawned much discussion examining the peril and potential of the quantified self movement and across numerous fields that will be mentioned in the following sections.

The COVID-19 pandemic has indeed engendered a new kind of biological come economic technological determinism that has brought forward not only imaginaries of resilient public spheres, such as mobilising on the basis of collective response (i.e vaccine development and urban solidarities in the beginning of the pandemic), but also an unfolding crisis of publicness and 'commoning' (Georgiou and Titley, 2022). All of which exacerbated pre-existing socio-economic forms of competitiveness (see vaccine nationalism), inequalities, polarisation and misinformation pathologies (Bratton, 2021). As communications scholars, Georgiou and Titley examined, the intense 'publicness' of the pandemic crisis invited reflection on progressive political possibilities, trust, transparency, accountability and democratic procedures, whilst also rendering visible that which is invisible, including collective precarity and dispossession (Georgiou and Titley, 2022). Such tensions bring forward forms of subjectification corresponding to new forms of material and biological complexity, as well as, we argue, complex sets of discourses integrated in human/data mediations.

This kind of complexity highlights a novel norm of significance in the link between biological life and the legitimation of biopolitical authority. Contrary to Blencowe's idealist form of plural authority, the pandemic put a closer connection between ideas of biological life for legitimising biopower; bound on an idealist-discursive determination of technology to create a near fetishisation of COVID-19 technologies. This exposed biological life to processes of objectification as either immunised or infected, vaccinated or unvaccinated, tracked and/or traced. In this sense, bodies and embodiment, as well as 'hyperreal' experiences (Bogard, 1996), became a focus point, or rather, an anchor of experience for Public Health Authorities and the tech companies that designed the infrastructures of COVID-19 technologies. Experiences of biological life thereby 'provide the anchorage', or the 'reference in objectivity', for a 'whole range of contemporary authoritative voices' ranging from the 'view of the market' through to 'medical expertise', as well as 'technological intelligence' (Blencowe, 2013, p. 11). To this end, we do agree that *being* biopolitically authoritative as Blencowe defined it, evokes 'a power and a citizenship practice that is used in the pursuit of a great spectrum of ends, which entails a plethora of exclusions and inequalities, and which frequently breaks down and gives way to new violence, domination and despotism' (Blencowe, 2013, p. 20).

To be biopolitically authoritative is to mediate experiences of life' to be a conduit to the force by which life (objectivity) pushes back (ibid, p. 20). Such a notion of biopolitical authority may indeed force us to rethink basic dynamics between the individual and society. In the neoliberal imaginaries of responsibilised societies comprised of self-governing individuals and technological consumers, the pandemic demands, as Georgiou and Titley (2022) put it, that we see ourselves as implicated in processes of transmission, and subject to forms of risk that cannot easily be individuate. Echoing Benjamin Bratton's 'epidemiological view of society' as an interdependent biological community that shifts 'our sense of subjectivity away from private individuation towards public transmissibility' (2021, p.393), we seek to unpack the discursive construction of the technological and its relationship with responsibilisation in biotracking culture, as well as the implications that this can have on biocitizenship. Our main question is thus centred around the ways in which sensory power creates new regimes of biopolitical authority, manifested in tech-solutionism regimes, clusters of responsibility and self-governance.

2. Methodological Framework

To address some of the components that answer this question, we deploy a discursive analytical technique that maps out examples across these themes. In the realm of policy making and policy shaping in which organisations like NHSX (the digital unit of the UK's National Health Service and the subsequent NHS Transformation Directorate), that dealt with numerous COVID-19 related technologies, including contact tracing apps, vaccine development and vaccine certificates, the importance of discourse becomes central as it exposes power relationships (Machin and Mayr, 2012, p. 10). As demonstrated in the COVID-19 response sections on the NHSX website between 2020–2021, rationales that have historically been used to propose the integration of technology in health, such as efficiency, economic accountability (cost effectiveness) and political accountability, were re-instrumentalised as antidotes to a 'global crisis'. 'Disruptive innovations' were put forward to manage the flow of the pandemic by means of restricting public transmissibility and biotracking mobility. Similarly, documents by the UK's Department of Health and Social Care relating to the NHS COVID-19 app and vaccine pass repeatedly communicated the pandemic using communitarian frames of transparency, community, collaboration, and 'improvement'. While the first three frames were used to mobilise the importance of accountability in public-private partnerships, 'improvement' was a frame that sought to respond to persistent public concerns about commercial gains and the consequences of third-party involvement regarding vaccine technology governance, as well as ethical concerns over privacy and surveillance (Ada Lovelace Institute, 2020b, 2021; Samuel and Lucivero, 2022).

While we scanned a large corpus of texts from official documents to press and stakeholder responses that render possible a selection for discourse-oriented content analysis, our study is more concerned with the ways in which COVID-19 technologies were promoted to *shape* public perceptions (and values) about pandemic management. We opted for a small sample of visual materials distributed by Public Health England to show how mediating and interfacial discursive strategies including the interlacing of graphic and textual cues, as well as 'meaning multiplication', all contributed to the promotion of tracking apps and vaccine passports (Bateman 2014 p. 6; Kress and Van Leeuwen, 2006; Wodak, 1989; 2001; Wodak and Meyer, 2009).

Adding to the mode of visual CDA, we use Norman Fairclough's three-part, or '3D', model to structure the analysis (2003). CDA works on three dimensions: the text itself (what it says), the order of discourse (how it relates to the other discourses shaping its particular domain, including the boundaries of the domains) and, finally, the social interactions it creates with the subjects of the domain (Young, 1981, p. 51). Attention to unequal power relations characterises the 'critical' dimension of CDA (Fairclough and Wodak, 1997). In this sense, we mobilise CDA in order to render explicit the hierarchies implicitly present in the visual discourses on responsibility within the context of the COVID-19 pandemic. Other references to key concepts, such as governance and efficiency of technologies, the adoption of apps, and 'public ethics narratives' surrounding transparency, accountability, consent and freedom that have emerged from existing studies in the UK and Europe (see Amann et al., 2021; Samuel and Lucivero, 2022) will also be threaded into our analysis.

3. Interfacing Tech Solutionism

Marketed as an efficient solution to the pandemic, COVID-19 technologies approached viral transmission as a problem to be tamed and optimised through algorithms and standardisation, evidencing a 'solutionist' mindset present throughout contemporary societies (Morozov, 2013, p.5). Capitalising on this formalisation of apps and platforms within society allowed the government to consequently normalise processes of biopolitical tracking (Lynskey, 2019; Ajana, 2021, p.10). Further to this, the normalisation of COVID-19 technologies have made visible tensions between public and private partnerships visible on a scale unlike ever before. As governments across the globe began to work with tech giants Apple and Google to create tracking apps, contention amongst the public surrounding their role arose.

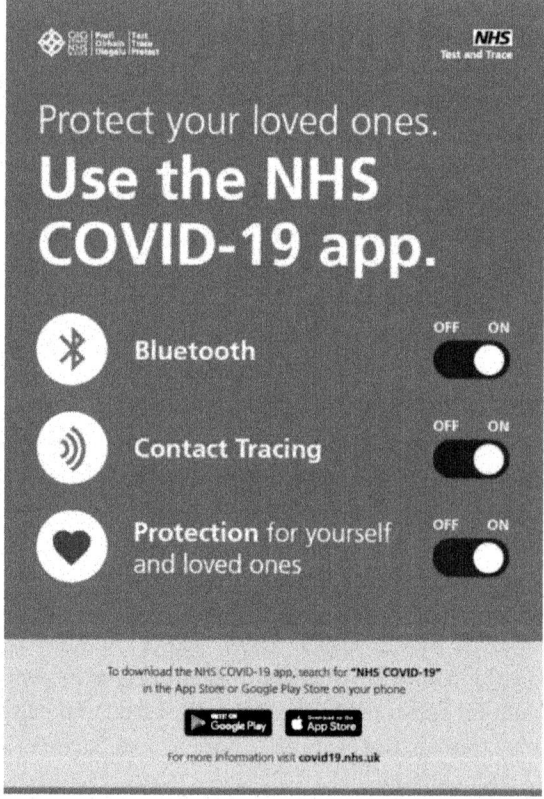

Fig. 1: Anon., 'Protect Your Loved Ones: Use the NHS COVID-19 App', 2020, source: Public Health England Coronavirus (COVID-19) Resource Centre

Image one demonstrates this tension when viewed as a 'meaningful whole' (Kress and Van Leeuwen, 2006, p.1) as the poster's use of intertextuality communicates complex ideological investment and responsibility rhetoric (Fig. 1). The ordering of the 'toggles' as a list suggest that 'protection' is a direct outcome to switching both bluetooth and contact tracing 'ON'. Thus, the toggle 'protection' informs the toggle 'ON' and vice versa. 'ON' represents the app, whilst 'protection' represents the supposed outcome, demonstrating the 'dialogicality' of the text bringing differing voices and styles together (Fairclough, 2003, p.41). Power, in a 'relational sense', is therefore communicated through the use of intertextuality as 'protection' and 'ON' inform, or 'relate', to one another. Technology is thereby presented as 'protection' through discursive composition and 'relationality' within the poster as it calls upon citizens to act accordingly. Through quite literally 'the switch of a button', protection of one's family is supposedly enabled, and the UK's track and trace app figures as a 'magical solution' to a complex problem echoing a tech and data-privileging mindset (Gilmore, 2021, p.383).

In addition, the image presents a further second layer whereby 'dialogicality' and materiality intersect. Bluetooth manifests a material and physical infrastructure of simulation that relies upon the distance and duration of interactions between individuals, determined from the strength of signals to communicate [ping] how risky an interaction is. Anonymised contact tracing information (IDs), distance and duration measurements, risk scores and other granulated data (including encrypted rolling proximity identifiers also called 'broadcast keys') became objects of intense debate in privacy lobbies and in public debates, resulting in updates on features to counter surveillance, preserve anonymity and restrict data viability on NHS cloud servers beyond fourteen days. While this points to the shortcomings between physical infrastructures of COVID-19 technologies and their ability to communicate across corporeal matter (bodies) and virtual spaces, it was also the first instance of biometric resistance. Bluetooth enabled devices transmit signals through hard surfaces and walls, rendering the proximity of the technology but not the users opaque. The 'pingdemic' (Bradshaw et al, 2021), a portmanteau ironic frame used in a flurry of memes during the summer of 2021, exposed such shortcomings, and was perhaps the first instance of exposing the disparities between virtual, simulated selves (Bogard, 1996), and the physical entities or embodied perceptions that they were meant to represent. During the pingdemic, the virtual self may be exposed to the virus within the *simulation* of the app, while the real body is not at risk, yet it is called to abide by a virtual responsibility akin to a gamified subject.

Another aspect manifested within image one is the public-private duality. The image includes the Google Play and Apple Store advertising. The 'relationality' between these logos and the COVID-19 pandemic thereby exemplifies a mixing of 'genres' (Fairclough, 2003, p.34; Weissenrieder and Fairclough, 1997, p.10). Through the commercial 'marketisation' of the app, 'healthcare' is presented as a business-like undertaking that needs to be actively promoted and sold (ibid). Thus, the 'mixing of genres' between healthcare and consumerism figures as a form of sensory power and governmentality. This mixing, or rather, 'chaining', is evidenced in the multimodality of the Google and Apple logo alongside language such as 'COVID-19' and 'protection'. The two genres (healthcare and consumerism) are presented alongside one other within the poster, leading to the 'hybridisation' of the two genres through assimilation (Fairclough, 2003, p.35). This hybridisation in turn 'blurs boundaries' between commercialism, business and health within contemporary social life, suggesting a new aesthetics of biopolitical authority.

Fig. 2: Anon., 'NHS Covid Pass accepted as EU Digital Covid Certificate equivalent', 2021, source: digitalhealth.net[1]

Datafication and self-tracking thus spilled over from the purely technological into the political, social and biological collectively during the pandemic. By conflating the 'purchase' of an app with adequate healthcare, the poster effectively utilised a 'hybridisation of genres' to systemically position individuals as consumers. As citizens began to reevaluate health in terms of risk and calculation, societies shifted away from a 'rights based welfare model of the citizen' to a 'citizen-consumer mode' (Peters, 2017, p.142). The digital biocitizen then increasingly became someone who understands health in relation to the market economy as the neoliberal state enforced new 'public–private partnerships' between the biological self and corporations, whilst the app, and crucially, its interface figured

---

1   Digital Health Net is a consultancy agency for NHSX and Public Health England, and a network infrastructure intelligence and public relations coordinator for every NHS Trust in the UK (https://www.digitalhealth.net/about-us/)

as mediator (ibid, p.138). Interestingly, in press coverage, Apple and Google were often positioned as both allies and obstacles to privacy (see, Samuel and Lucivero, 2022), but a lack of clarity on the nature of partnerships between the NHS, the British government and other Big Tech and data processing companies (including Palantir, Faculty, and Amazon), became an object of public scrutiny among those that sought to call biopolitical authority into account (Ruhaak, 2020)[2].

Image two, and its associated context (*Digital Health* press release, part of a nationwide PR campaign) is one of a myriad, almost identical images, circulated by UK-based NHS trusts, government departments and the press during the summer of 2021 (Fig. 2). It highlights the tensions surrounding the role and function of COVID-19 technologies, as alternatives to easing local lock-downs and enabling cross-border crossings. Initially intended as proof of vaccination for entry (i.e. 'pass') into social spaces like pubs, cafes, concerts and restaurants, COVID-19 passes were soon also used for travelling; taking them from purely domestic realms into international ones too. COVID-19 passes then became 'COVID-19 passports' depending on the context in which they were used. Here, the imagery and phraseology used in *Digital Health's* press release (and nationwide PR campaign reaching mainstream press and thousands of NHS trusts), implies a kind of governmentality steeped in state-sponsored views on collectivism and 'foreignness', whereby use of the word 'certificate' and 'passport' conflates with notions of borders, distinction and separateness. In this way COVID-19 passes spilled over from their originally intended purpose to take on a new role as a COVID-19 *passport*, part of a visual communications apparatus that attempted to conceal new political and social tensions. Under a guise of ease and interoperability, COVID-19 passes transitioned into COVID-19 passports with debates around the transparency vs opacity of private data coming to light.

The positioning of the small rectangular protrusion concealing the biometric RFID chip in the passport underneath the QR code of the Vaccine Pass App may also reveal this pretext. QR codes for vaccine passes manifest this tension as individuals were prompted to continually 'check-in' to locations, events and activities, as well as across borders. The QR code [Quick Response] aesthetic, as well as the rapid access control system akin to biometric technologies used for user identification, labelling and product stocking, act as a social metaphor (Bateman, 2014) for credentialing relationships between 'immune' subjects, public health checkers, merchants and border control securities. In this way, 'responsible' and 'healthy' citizens were implied to be those who actively engaged in self-monitoring and self-tracking through QR 'check-ins', whilst social risks, such as ill health, were increasingly reconfigured as 'self care' rather than the responsibility of the state (Lemke, 2001, p. 201). As tech fetishisation flourished, digital technology rapidly

---

2 Ruhaak, A, 2020. An open letter to government: https://medium.com/@anouk ruhaak/open-letter-b7cb79832064.

became the default way to conduct life. The physical act of entering a social space then became digitally stored through check-ins and QR codes, creating not only a digital record of personal information, numbers and text, but also of experience and behaviour.

3.1 Encoding Capitalised Tracking

Within the context of medicine, public health, and epidemiology in particular, there has been a long history of surveillant practices in monitoring the outbreak and reproduction rate of diseases including influenza (Cheng et al, 2011), smallpox (Henderson, 1976), and ebola (Milinovich, Magalhaes and Hu, 2014). Furthermore, the fetishisation and normalisation of digital technologies has facilitated mass surveillance across societies to enable 'governing from afar' without the need for 'constant direct observation or containment' (Graham, and Wood, 2003, p.228).

However, the COVID-19 pandemic presented a critical juncture in the history of surveillant practices as COVID-19 technologies departed from mere disease surveillance alone to categorisation and organisation of individuals at both a micro and macro scale. In their capacity to predict the transmission of coronavirus, track and trace apps and vaccine passports can be defined as 'predictive' or 'preemptive' technologies. Due to the virus' lengthy incubation period, as well as the risk that many individuals can be asymptomatic whilst carrying the virus, meant that the app's ability to predict potential cases and 'hotspots' meant intercepting and influencing mobility first at an individual level and then as part of a collective. In other words, COVID-19 technologies were less concerned with the act of surveilling, but with the act of ultimately influencing and modifying behaviour to enact governmentality for the sake of the greater good.

Therefore, a key tension operationalised by COVID-19 technologies is between the individual and collective. If we are to heed responsibilisation as a form of governmentality, then the objective is to align individuals to certain sociopolitical standards by acting accordingly to demonstrate a 'conduct of conduct' (Foucault, 2003, p.186). In other words, through responsibilisation rhetoric, tracking apps and COVID-19 passports discursively invited individuals to carry out 'governance over others' as well as 'self-governance' (Juhila, Raitakari and Hall, 2017, p.2). Within advanced liberal societies individuals 'regulate their own behaviour to ensure it is consonant with the interests of the state' (Pierson, 2004, p.75). Therefore, sensory power during the pandemic depended on 'responsible actors' to act accordingly with one another through QR codes, check-ins and clicks for the 'betterment' of society. Such governmental techniques then 'work on both the level of the individual and the level of the population' (Peeters, 2019, p.52).

Fig. 3: Anon., 'CORONAVIRUS: SELF-ISOLATE WHEN ALERTED', 2020, source: Public Health England Coronavirus (COVID-19) Resource Centre

Image three uses emotive and directive language to emphasise this tension between the individual and collective as viewers are told to 'play one's part' in society (Fig. 3). Here, 'assumption' is a key mechanism deployed to exert power (Fairclough, 2003, p.40). In this way, discourse is revealed through that which is unsaid or absent (Machin and Mayr, 2012, p.2). The text *assumes* that 'playing one's part' is a necessary moral duty of citizens, thereby creating a 'value system' typical of 'neoliberal economic and political discourse' (Fairclough, 2003, p.58). That is, being a 'good biocitizen' means one should assume responsibility by downloading the app in line with a neoliberal desire for societal 'efficiency and adaptability' (ibid). Albeit absent and 'unsaid', this 'assumption' based on the act of 'downloading' evokes a 'moral duty' of 'hegemonic and universally understood' responsibility (Fairclough, 2003, p.40).

This kind of language that aims to moralise 'alertness' then demonstrates how responsibilisation has colonised so much of our social fabric, including healthcare and social policy, that it now impacts how we take care of ourselves and one another (Brown and Baker, 2013, p.1). Processes of responsibilisation take place not through coercion, but through the exhortation and assumption that citizens should 'undertake a variety of personal disciplines to manage themselves' centred upon expert advice dispensed by public health bodies and government agencies (ibid, p.3). Through discourse such as 'play your part', individuals are tactfully positioned as rational decision-makers in charge of managing one's own (as well as others) fate, ultimately ignoring complex socio-economic factors that impact one's ability and financial capacity to safely self-isolate or own a smartphone.

Furthermore, the framing of responsibilisation took place discursively through imagery as well as text during the pandemic as images of QR codes, interfaces, tracking apps and code were all media forms employed to communicate responsibilisation rhetoric. Thus, taking into account the visual 'public ethics narrative' that surrounded tracking apps and vaccine passports (Samuel and Lucivero, 2022, p.4), a further tension arose around whether such technologies should be made voluntary or mandatory. Fervent debate ensued throughout the UK pertaining to the ethical dimensions of making such technologies compulsory, whilst others argued it a necessary step out of lockdown.

In an open debate published by *The Guardian* in 2021 about the introduction of vaccine passports, one member of the public proclaimed that 'some freedoms have to be tempered by an overriding social responsibility which occasionally needs to be legally enforced' (Winnick et al, 2021). Here, emphasis is again on individual responsibility as part of a societal collective, but it is interesting to note that the individual mentions legal enforcement *if* individuals do not first comply with societies' tacit moral obligations. Responsibilisation then figures first as a choice, with law enforcement considered a 'last resort' and presented as a 'threat' to those who do not choose 'correctly'. Thus 'choice' in this context figures cautionary as individuals not only face a potential reward for the outcome of their decision, but also a potential risk. To be irresponsible within the eyes of societies' neoliberal standards would mean taking a risk and being deemed 'risky' with potential personal consequences. Therefore, the risk of being shamed publicly, as well as the perceived 'threat to personal control' (Pyysiäinen et al, 2017, p.217), became a communicative tool to enact governmentality and enforce responsibilisation.

Conversely, others argued that although inevitable, mandatory digital vaccine passes posed a threat to privacy with one user claiming 'to avoid fear of commercial misuse of personal data, the system should not be run by a commercial body' (Winnick et al, 2021). Here, the individual is more concerned with *who* is governing such a documentation system rather than whether it is made mandatory or not. Similar concerns were echoed in several European newspapers over the trustworthiness of Apple and Google and their commitment to data protection (Amann, Sleigh, Vayena, 2021, p.8). The national German Newspaper *Die Welt* emphasised that Apple and Google were 'not democratically legitimised' highlighting the complex technopolitical dimensions associated with COVID-19 technologies and their rapid roll-out (ibid). COVID-19 technologies thus presented a unique conundrum to the field of surveillance ethics because in their capacity to measure, predict, track and regulate pathogens, they cluster modulated behaviours of bodies (Isin and Rupert, 2020, p. 8). Technologies, like vaccine passports and tracking apps, then become an intermediary media form of identity 'legitimation' as such systems are assigned ultimate political and social power (Castells, 1997, p.8). Those who do not, or physically cannot submit their biometric data, are ultimately denied access to certain rights and freedoms on account of their 'biovalue' (Rose and Novas, 2005, p.29).

One may ask what these tensions mean for formalising new norms for biocitizenship and identity beyond just being 'instrumentalized by biopower' (Happe, Johnson, & Levina, 2018, p.4). Referring to the long and complicated relationship that biology and the body has had with power, identity and belonging helps us to understand the potential implications of biocitizenship. Thus, it is this convergence of 'bio' and 'citizenship' that signals a problematic nationalistic and colonial past (Gillham, 2001; Grodin, Miller, Kelly, 2018) where individuals have either been 'included' or 'excluded'.

3.2 Biopolitices/Biocitizenship/Bioprotection

Track and trace apps and vaccine passports are forms of biotechnology that take the human body and its viral status to determine one's mobility and potential level of 'risk', ultimately partaking in a 'politics of protection' (Ajana, 2013, p.52). The somatic body becomes informationalised and abstracted within a web of networked data and knowledge as the body and one's health status is monitored and stored. A politics of protection thus 'curiously straddles both the logic of inclusion and exclusion' (ibid). This is evidenced in the closing of borders and hasty lockdowns across the globe to prevent the virus entering from 'high risk' countries. This situational and physical dimension of track and trace apps and vaccine passports, as well as attitudes towards the virus overall, thus dangerously veers into a politics of protection over who does and does not properly 'belong' (Zylinska, 2004, p.526). 'Othering' became legitimised as the perceived threat of residual otherness is 'regulated and contained with the aim to facilitate the exercise of freedom for those who qualify as 'belonging' citizens (Ajana, 2013, p.129). The body thus became vulnerable to extractive operations of technological regulation and control steeped in ideological, political and racial dimensions hidden under the guise of 'science' or 'public safety'.

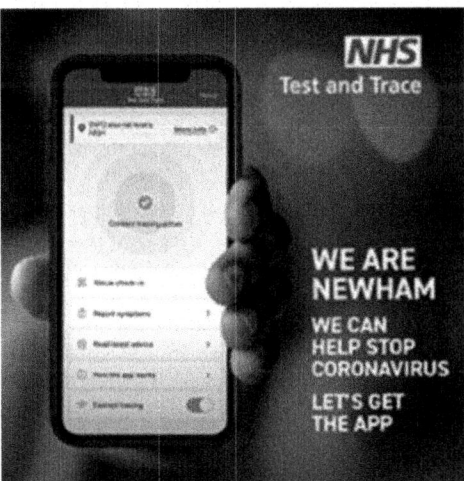

Fig. 4: Anon., 'WE ARE NEWHAM',
2020, source: Public Health England
Coronavirus (COVID-19) Resource Centre

Image four simultaneously demonstrates this tension of mobility between inclusion/exclusion through both text and photographic imagery (Fig. 4). The smartphone seen within the image shows the UK track and trace app screen, which is held forthright in the foreground by a figure blurred in a background of concentric bubbles, potentially figuring as a social metaphor for 'protection bubbles'. Furthermore, the text seen to the right of the image is direct in its call to action as bold, capitalised font states 'WE ARE NEWHAM' and 'LET's GET THE APP'. Viewed separately, both the text and photograph would make sense, but when taken together, they create a message of urgency to use the app.

First, use of the word 'WE' invokes a nationalistic tone similar in style to a call to arms poster. A notable comparison would be the Lord Kitchener 'Your country needs YOU' poster of 1914, which was turned into a recruitment poster for the first world war (Ginzburg, 2001). By utilising the 'war metaphor' to encourage users to download the app, it confronts us with urgency and instruction (Sabucedo, Alzate and Hur, 2020). Although metaphors can make unfamiliar and unprecedented situations, like the pandemic, feel somewhat familiar, invoking the war metaphor is wholly problematic. To be at war is not a positive, no matter how much the heroic and noble imaginary is invoked (Lohmeyer and Taylor, 2020). The war metaphor invites 'identification of the enemy' (Sabucedo, Alzate and Hur, 2020, p.619), yet the enemy is a virus, and viruses and bacteria exist everywhere. To be at war with a virus is to be at war with biology, and it is this framing of biology as something to be feared that led to fear of an 'invisible enemy'. This fear only exacerbated anxieties about the pandemic in general as people became increasingly afraid of the world and natural bacteria around them.

Furthermore, repetition of the word 'WE' in the poster suggests notions of a 'collective struggle', which can be unpacked using Fairclough's approach on 'styles' (Fairclough, 2003, p.159). 'styles' can be defined as 'discoursal aspects of ways of being', or simply, identity, identities and identification (ibid). Within the context of the poster, 'we' is the 'style' being discussed, as the word invites a process of identification as part of a collective. The use of collective language here then invites identification of a 'social identity', that is, a process of identification in relation to others as part of a community (i.e. Newham) (ibid, p.160).

As a borough within inner East London, use of the name 'Newham' alongside repetition of the word, or 'style', 'WE', suggests communal responsibility and a moral duty to oneself and others to download the app. Responsibilisation centres less on the individual here, but more on the collective responsibility of a community, thus capitalising on the identity of those who feel that they belong to the Newham community. However, Newham is one of the poorest boroughs in London with 49 % of households living in poverty, and 52 % of children growing up in low-income households (Newham Council, 2020). As a result, digital exclusion is rife within the borough as around 11,000 people are left without internet access because they cannot afford it (Samuel, 2021). This digital divide existed before the pandemic, but coronavirus only widened the divide as remote working and learning came into effect. Thus, in claiming 'WE ARE NEWHAM', the poster only serves to further exclude those without internet access, a smartphone, or the financial wherewithal to participate in contemporary consumerist culture.

As one of the poorest boroughs in London, the name 'Newham' alongside 'we' invites the social identification of individuals as part of a working-class group. In other words, it appeals to the communal ethics of social obligation by communicating neoliberal ideology at the 'collective level' (Fairclough, 2003, p.160). Thus, the poster exploits the identities of working-class citizens in Newham by capitalising on a sense of collective struggle and hardship to promote the app. In so doing, the poster operates under a mirage of care and unification, whilst systemic issues pertaining to welfare and poverty were sidelined.

Health and social inequalities were exacerbated during the pandemic, drawing further divides and injustice among those who could 'stay at home' to exercise 'responsibility' whilst 'averting risks and adopting health protecting behaviours' (Cardona, 2020, p.1), whilst others had less agency and could not afford to do so. For instance, such discourses of 'protection' and digitally mediated safety did little to address the perils of women isolating in violent homes, the freedom of migrants detained in the name of public health, and many urban poor forced to navigate scarce access to basic provisions (Georgiou and Titley, 2022, p. 337; Alim, 2020; Ada Lovelace Institute, 2020b).

An article in *WIRED* magazine discusses the introduction of the UK's vaccine passport in 2021, referring to it, similarly, as a 'de facto digital passport to freedom' (Stokel-Walker, 2021). Here, the choice of language suggests the degree of power vaccine passports held in determining one's mobility and rights. Passports have a long-running and complex history in relation to nationalism, identity and citizenship as 'belonging' is increasingly politicised over one's economic and biological 'contribution' or 'productivity' to society (Mavelli, 2018, p.1). Here, vaccine passports carry similar political weighting as they determine one's ability to travel across states, borders and boundaries depending on one's vaccination status.

Such forms of governmentality result in inclusion and exclusion of individuals on account of their 'bio-economic factor' (Ajana, 2012, p.862). That is, those who pose 'risk' to the health of a nation (both financially and biologically) are prevented from partaking in social spaces or accessing certain services despite one's personal circumstance or narrative. A notable example of this was Australia's sudden border closure to citizens returning from India without any forewarning, leaving thousands stranded abroad whilst the pandemic ravaged India (Anon, BBC News, 2021). As the world progressed towards a politics of protection and defence during the pandemic, track and trace apps and vaccine passports enforced the technological mediation of bodies through measurement, quantification, tracking, abstraction, nudging and interfaces, which fundamentally challenged 'the concept of what we understand life, the natural and humanness to mean' (Blackman, 2008, p.2).

Order and rule became internalised through technologies as biopower was exerted over human activities 'at the most detailed, individual level' (Foucault, 2003, p.7). That is, surveillance of the body took place through the continuous logging of movement, check-ins and 'tagging'. This in turn created an illusion of having control whilst sensory power 'relentlessly and voraciously tracked and traced our movements, desires and needs' (Isin and Rupert, 2020, p.12). As individuals became responsibilised through surveillance; macro-level, reform-based solutions to social issues were ultimately discarded in favour of 'carefully delineated action by atomised individuals' (Morozov, 2013, p.237). This effectively lead individuals to feel not only responsible for themself, but for the rest of society also as sensory power was enacted over sick and healthy clusters.

These 'techniques of power' thus evidence a form of 'state control of the biological' (Foucault, 2003, p.239). Biopower, and as a consequence biopolitical authority, was exerted over individuals to 'be responsible' whilst sickness and the body became politicised. Within the responsibilisation rhetoric, to fall sick with coronavirus suggested selfishness or irresponsibility over others' wellbeing. It is this exact rhetoric that was widely adopted during the pandemic as the fate of one's health was viewed as the personal responsibility of individuals and their devices.

Yet, the pandemic resurfaced a novel crisis on public trust towards biopower (Ada Lovelace Institute, 2020a) as forms of identification and imagination proportional to its material and biological complexity were produced. This re-animated forms of displacement, scepticism, resistance and denial (e.g. pingdemic, data ethics advocacy and anti vaccers) under conditions of complex and contingent publicness (Georgou and Tetley, 2022). This may indeed drive further forms of scepticism and invite public debates, resistance and denial, not only in relation to being subjects of governance and informed expertise, but also in relation to exposing relations of interdependence and solidarity.

4. Conclusion

This paper sought to advance a theory of sensory power in relation to tracking apps and vaccine passports by arguing that such devices enact a novel form of governance. Central to our argument is the governmentality of such technologies through not only their visual aspects (design, layout, imagery, symbols), but also their embodied aspects (clicks, shares, saves, check-ins). We evidence this through critically dissecting various adverts, posters and articles that represent and/or discuss tracking apps and vaccine passports using critical discourse analysis. The visual and discursive samples utilised in this paper therefore seek to demonstrate the communicative power linked to the promotion and adoption of tracking apps and vaccine passports as they produced novel regimes of 'live' authority of the self and others in continual feedback.

Through this continuum of tracking, sharing, tapping, checking in, nudging and alerting, experiential phenomena such as going to a cafe, restaurant or shop, became encoded into datafied information amenable to algorithmic extraction and abstraction. This accumulation of 'lively' (Lupton, 2016, p.114) data thus assimilated experiential phenomena into a networked assemblage of information. This consequently facilitated the accumulation of 'subject peoples' (making multiplicities of people useful, healthy and productive) and the accumulation of capital (generating economic, cultural, social capital and transforming them into wealth) [which] also required the accumulation of knowledge (about objects and subjects of power) appropriate to these forms' (Isin and Ruppert, 2020, p. 3).

Through a multidisciplinary methodological approach, this paper highlighted the specific tensions and themes that arose from the adoption of tracking apps and vaccine passports. Specifically, technological fetishisation and the intended role and function of apps and devices vs their 'interoperable' use, private vs public relationships, capitalised tracking and the responsibilisation of individuals vs the collective, and finally, biopolitics and dynamics of protection/defence, care/control and inclusion/exclusion that determined the rights and mobility of individuals as either belonging 'biocitizens' or undesirable 'others'.

Furthermore, 'methodology' was adopted over the term 'method' as we utilised a 'theory driven process' whereby new objects of research were constructed in relation to topics as they presented themselves to us (i.e. the pandemic, shifting power dynamics, and the use of tracing apps and vaccine passports) rather than opting for the 'selection and application of pre-established methods' (Fairclough, 2010, p.5). In doing so, this paper highlighted the 'lively' nature of data monitoring and tracking that intervenes and influences behaviour in a preemptive, predictive and 'continuous' manner in perpetual flux.

Through exploration into how authority and clusters of responsibilisation are visually and textually framed, this paper demonstrated the aesthetic power of tracking apps and vaccine passports that paved the way for novel forms of governmentality rooted in responsibilisation. To be a 'healthy and responsible' citizen became a civic duty as instances of coughing into one's elbow, wearing a mask and carrying hand sanitiser and antibacterial wipes all signified good 'bio-practice' (Kolopenuk, 2020, p.24). Self-tracking practices thereby facilitated new modes of being, expressing and communicating through visual cues and modified behaviour as a pervading belief that being able to change things is by getting humans to 'behave in more responsible and sustainable ways to maximise efficiency' (Morozov, 2013, p.x).

To this end, tracking apps and vaccine passports signify a novel form of governmentality rooted in networked relations and *relationality*. That is, the nature of these devices, both in their design and function, have made it easier to see oneself more as a node in a biopolitical network to which one is responsible, rather than as an autonomous individual whose sovereignty is guaranteed by free will (Bratton, 2021, p.405).

References

Ada Lovelace Institute. 2020a. "Confidence in a crisis? Building public trust in a contact tracing app." [online report] Available at: https://www.adalovelaceinstitute.org/report/confidence-in-crisis-building-public-trust-contact-tracing-app/

Ada Lovelace Institute. 2021. "The data divide."[online article] Available at: https://www.adalovelaceinstitute.org/report/the-data-divide/

Ada Lovelace Institute. 2021. "What place should COVID-19 vaccine passports have in society? Findings from a rapid expert deliberation chaired by Professor Sir Jonathan Montgomery." [online article] Ada Lovelace Institute. Available at: https://www.adalovelaceinstitute.org/summary/covid-19-vaccine-passports/

Ajana, B. 2010. "Recombinant Identities: Biometrics and Narrative Bioethics." *Journal of Bioethical Inquiry.* Vol.7; Issue:2, pp.237–258.

Ajana, B. 2012. "Biometric Citizenship." *Citizenship Studies.* Vol.16; Issue: 7, pp.85–870.

Ajana, B. 2013. *Governing through Biometrics: The Biopolitics of Identity.* London: Palgrave Macmillan.

Ajana, B. 2017. "Digital Health and the Biopolitics of the Quantified Self." *Digital Health.* Vol. 3; Issue: 1, pp.1–18.

Ajana, B. 2020. "Personal metrics: Users' experiences and perceptions of self-tracking practices and data." *Social Science Information,* 59, 654–678.

Ajana, B. 2021. "Immunitarianism: defence and sacrifice in the politics of Covid-19." *History and Philosophy of the Life Sciences.* Vol. 43; pp.1–31.

Alevizou, G. 2017. "From digital commons to the data-fied urge: Theorising evolving trends in the intersections of digital culture and open education." *First Monday,* Vol.22; No.6.

Alevizou, G. 2021. "Civic Media and Technologies of Belonging: where digital citizenship and the 'right to the city' converge." *International Journal of Media and Cultural Policy.* Vol. 16, No.3, pp. 269–290.

Alim, A .2020. "Food for London Now: '1 in 5 children short of food'." *Evening Standard,* 9 December 2020. Available at: https://www.standard.co.uk/news/foodforlondon/food-for-london-now-children-food-shortage-b232967.html.

Amann, J., Sleigh, J., Vayena, E. 2021. "Digital contact-tracing during the Covid-19 pandemic: An analysis of newspaper coverage in Germany, Austria, and Switzerland." *PLoS ONE.* Vol.16; Issue: 2.

Anon. 2021. "Australia's Indian ban criticised as 'racist' rights breach" [online article]. Available: https://www.bbc.co.uk/news/world-australia-56967520 [Accessed 06/05/2021].

Barnett, C., N. Clarke, P., Cloke & Malpass, A. 2008. "The elusive subjects of neoliberalism: Beyond the analytics of governmentality." *Cultural Studies.* Vol. 22, No.5: pp. 624–653.

Benjamin, R. 2013. *People's Science: Bodies and Rights on the Stem Cell Frontier.* California: Stanford University.

Benkler, Y. 2006. *The wealth of networks: How social production transforms markets and freedom*. New Haven, Conn.: Yale University Press.

Blackman, L. 2008. *The Body: The Key Concepts*. Oxfordshire: Routledge.

Blencowe, C. 2013. "Biopolitical authority, objectivity and the groundwork of modern citizenship." *Journal of Political Power*, Vol. 6. Issue: 1, pp. 9–28.

Bogard, W. 1996. *The Simulation of Surveillance: Hyper-Control in Telematic Societies*. Cambridge: The Press Syndicate.

Bradschaw, T., Pickard, J, Sheppard, D. 2021. "UK 'pingdemic' spreads as record 600,000 people told to self-isolate" [online article]. *BBC News*. Available: https://www.ft.com/content/1bdef6b5-672d-46e0-9502-492a432a51af [Accessed 06/08/2021].

Bratton, BH. 2021. *The Revenge of the Real: Politics for a Post-pandemic World*. London: Verso.

Brown, B. 2014. "Will Work For Free: The Biopolitics of Unwaged Digital Labour. tripleC: Communication, Capitalism & Critique." *Global Sustainable Information Society*, Vol. 12.

Brown, B. J. & Baker, S. 2013. *Responsible Citizens: Individuals, Health and Policy under Neoliberalism*. London: Anthem Press.

Cardona, B. 2020. "The pitfalls of personalization rhetoric in time of health crisis: COVID-19 pandemic and cracks on neoliberal ideologies." in *Health Promotion International*. Vol. 36; Issue: 3, pp. 714–721.

Castells, M. 1997. *The Power of Identity*. New Jersey: Blackwell Publishers, Inc.

Castells, M. 2009. *Communication Power*. Oxford: Oxford University Press

Castells, M. 2012. *Networks of outrage and hope: social movements on the internet*. Cambridge: Polity.

Cheng, C. K., Ip, D. K., Cowling, B. J., Ho, L. M., Leung, G. M. & Lau, E. H. 2011. Digital Dashboard Design Using Multiple Data Streams for Disease Surveillance with Influenza Surveillance as an Example. *Journal of Medical Internet Research*, Vol.13; Issue: 85.

Chouliarki, L. & Fairclough, N. 1999. *Discourse in late modernity: Rethinking critical discourse analysis*. Edinburgh: Edinburgh University Press.

Couldry, N. Mejias, UA. "Data Colonialism: Rethinking Big Data's Relation to the Contemporary Subject." *Television & New Media*. Vol. 20. Issue 4, pp. 336–349.

Davies, B. 2021. "'Personal Health Surveillance': The Use of mHealth in Healthcare Responsibilisation." *Public Health Ethics*. Oxford: Oxford Academic.

Dijk, T. A. V. 1983. *Strategies of discourse comprehension*. New York: Academic Press.

Du, L., Raposos, V. L. & Wang, M. 2020. "COVID-19 Contact Tracing Apps: A Technologic Tower of Babel and the Gap for International Pandemic Control." *JMIR Mhealth Uhealth*. Vol. 8, e23194.

Fairclough, N. 2003. *Analysing Discourse: Textual Analysis for Social Research*. London and New York: Routledge.

Fairclough, N. 2010. *Critical Discourse Analysis: The Critical Study of Language*, London: Taylor & Francis Group.

Fairclough, N. A. W., R 1997. *Discourse as social interaction: Discourse studies: A multidisciplinary introduction. Vol. 2,* Thousand Oaks. California: Sage Publications.

Foucault, M. 1980. *Power/Knowledge: Selected Interviews and Other Writings.* New York: Pantheon Books.

Foucault, M. 1982. "The Subject and Power." *Critical Inquiry.* Vol.8; Issue: 4; pp.777–795.

Foucault, M. 2003. *Society must be defended: lectures at the Collège de France, 1975–76,* 1st ed. New York: Picador.

Gee, J. P. & Handford, M. 2012. *The Routledge Handbook of Discourse Analysis.* London: Taylor & Francis Group.

Georgiou, M & Titley, G. "Publicness and commoning: Pandemic intersections and collective visions at times of crisis." *International Journal of Cultural Studies.* Vol. 25. pp. 331–348.

Gillham, N. W. 2001. "Sir Francis Galton and the birth of eugenics." *Annual Review Genetics,* Vol. 35, pp. 83–101.

Gilmore, J. N. 2021. "Predicting Covid-19: wearable technology and the politics of solutionism." *Cultural Studies.* Vol.35; pp. 382–391.

Ginzburg, C. 2001. "'Your Country Needs You': A Case Study in Political Iconography." *History Workshop Journal.* Vol. 52, pp. 1–22.

Graham, S and WOOD, D. 2003. "Digitizing Surveillance: Categorisation, Space, Inequality." *Critical Social Policy.* Vol, 23; Issue: 2.

Grodin, M. A., Miller, E. L. & Kelly, J. I. 2018. "The Nazi Physicians as Leaders in Eugenics and 'Euthanasia': Lessons for Today." *American journal of public health.* Vol. 108, pp. 53–57.

Happe, K., Johnson, J., & Levina, M. (EDS.) 2018. *Biocitizenship: The Politics of Bodies, Governance, and Power.* New York: New York University Press.

Henderson, D. A. 1976. "Surveillance of Smallpox." *International Journal of Epidemiology.* Vol. 5, pp. 19–28.

Isin, E. & Ruppert, E. 2020. "The Birth of Sensory Power: How a Pandemic Made it Visible?" *Big Data & Society.* Vol. 7, Issue: 2; pp. 1–15.

Juhila, K. & Raitakari, S. 2017. *Responsibilisation at the Margins of Welfare Services.* London: Routledge.

Kelion, L. 2021. "NHS Covid-19 app update blocked for breaking Apple and Google's rules." [online article] *BBC News.* Available: https://www.bbc.co.uk/news/technology-56713017 [Accessed 03/05/2021].

Kitchin R. 2014. "Big data, new epistemologies and paradigm shifts." *Big Data Society.* Vol.1, pp. 1–12.

Kloppenburg, S. & van der Ploeg, I. 2018. "Securing Identities: Biometric Technologies and the Enactment of Human Bodily Differences." *Science as Culture.* Vol. 29, pp. 57–76.

Kolopenuk, J. 2020. "Provoking Bad Biocitizenship." *Hastings Center Report,* Vol.50; Issue: 1, pp.23–29.

Kress, G. & Leeuwen, T. V. 2006. *Reading images: the grammar of visual design*. London: Routledge.

Leith, D. J. & Farrell, S. 2021. "Measurement-based evaluation of Google/Apple Exposure Notification API for proximity detection in a commuter bus." *PLOS ONE*, Vol. 16.

Lemke, T. 2001. "'The birth of bio-politics': Michel Foucault's lecture at the Collège de France on neo-liberal governmentality." *Economy and Society*. Vol. 30, pp. 190–207.

Lohmeyer, B. A. & Taylor, N. 2021. "War, Heroes and Sacrifice: Masking Neoliberal Violence During the COVID-19 Pandemic." *Critical Sociology*. Vol. 47; pp. 625–639.

Lupton, D. 2014. "The commodification of patient opinion: the digital patient experience economy in the age of big data." *Sociology of Health and Illness*, Vol. 36, pp. 856–69.

Lupton, D. 2016. "The diverse domains of quantified selves: self-tracking modes and dataveillance." *Economy and Society*. Vol. 45, Issue: 1, pp. 101–122.

Lynskey, D. 2019. "'Alexa, are you invading my privacy?' – the dark side of our voice assistants." [online article] Available: https://www.theguardian.com/technology/2019/oct/09/alexa-are-you-invading-my-privacy-the-dark-side-of-our-voice-assistants [Accessed 03/04/2021].

Machin, D. & Mayr, A. 2012. *How to Do Critical Discourse Analysis: A Multimodal Introduction*. London: SAGE Publications.

Mavelli, L. 2017. "Governing the resilience of neoliberalism through biopolitics." *European Journal of International Relations*, Vol. 23, pp. 489–512.

Mavelli, L. 2018. "Citizenship for Sale and the Neoliberal Political Economy of Belonging." *International Studies Quarterly*. Vol 62, Issue 3, pp. 482–493.

McGregor, S. 2001. "Neoliberalism and health care." *International Journal of Consumer Studies*. Vol. 25, pp. 82–89.

Milkan, S. 2020. "Techno-solutionism and the standard human in the making of the COVID-19 pandemic." *Big Data & Society*, Vol. 7.

Milinovich, G. J., Magalhães, R. J. S. & HU, W. 2015. "Role of big data in the early detection of Ebola and other emerging infectious diseases." *The Lancet Global Health*, Vol. 3.

Miller, B. 2020. "Is Technology Value-Neutral?" *Science, Technology, & Human Values*. Vol. 46, pp. 53–80.

Morozov, E. 2013. *To save everything, click here: the folly of technological solutionism*. New York: Public Affairs.

Morozov, E. 2013. "We are abandoning all the checks and balances." [online article] *The Guardian*. Available: https://www.theguardian.com/technology/2013/mar/09/evgeny-morozov-technology-solutionism-interview [Accessed 21/06/2021].

Newham Council. 2020. "Towards a Better Newham" online council webpage]. Available: https://www.newham.gov.uk/news/article/541/-towards-a-better-newham-action-plan-approved-to-support-the-borough-s-recovery-during-covid-19- [Accessed 02/04/2021].

Noble, S, U. 2018. *Algorithms of Oppression*. New York: New York University Press.

Nonhoff, M. 2017. "Discourse analysis as critique." *Palgrave Communications,* Vol. 3.

Peeters, R. 2019. "Manufacturing Responsibility: The Governmentality of Behavioural Power in Social Policies." *Social Policy and Society.* Vol. 18; pp. 51–65.

Peeters, R. & Schuilenburg, M. 2017. "The birth of mindpolitics: understanding nudging in public health policy." *Social Theory & Health.* Vol. 15, pp. 138–159.

Peters, M. 2001. "Education, enterprise culture and the entrepreneurial self: A Foucauldian perspective." *Journal of Educational Enquiry.* No. 2: pp. 58–71.

Peters, M. A. 2017. "From State responsibility for education and welfare to self-responsibilisation in the market." *Discourse: Studies in the Cultural Politics of Education.* Vol. 38; pp. 138–145.

Petersen, A. 2018. *Digital Health and Technological Promise*. London: Routledge.

Petersen, A., Schermuly, A. C. & Anderson, A. 2019. "The shifting politics of patient activism: From bio-sociality to bio-digital citizenship." *Health: An Interdisciplinary Journal for the Social Study of Health, Illness and Medicine.* Vol. 23, pp. 478–494.

Pierson, C. 2004. *The Modern State*. London and New York: Routledge.

Pink, S & Fors, V. 2017. "Being in a mediated world: self-tracking and the mind-body-environment." *Cultural Geographies.* Vol. 24. Issue: 3, pp. 375–38.

Porter, T. M. 1995. *Trust in Numbers: The Pursuit of Objectivity in Science and Public Life*. New Jersey: Princeton University Press.

Public Health England. 2021. "Coronavirus (COVID-19) Resource Centre" [Online webpage]. [online webpage]: *HM Government: Public Health England*. Available: https://coronavirusresources.phe.gov.uk/ [Accessed 18/02/2021].

Pyysiäinen, J., Halpin, D. & Guilfoyle, A. 2017. "Neoliberal governance and 'responsibilization' of agents: reassessing the mechanisms of responsibility-shift in neoliberal discursive environments." *Distinktion: Journal of Social Theory.* Vol. 18; pp. 215–235.

Rose, N. 1992. "Governing the enterprising self." *The values of the enterprise culture: The moral debate,* ed. P. Heelas and P. Morris, pp. 141–164. London: Routledge.

Rose, N. & Miller, P. 1992. "Political Power beyond the State: Problematics of Government." *The British Journal of Sociology.* Vol. 43; pp. 173–205.

Rose, N and Carlos, N. 2005. "Biological citizenship." In *Global assemblages: Technology, politics and ethics as anthropological problems*. (Eds) Aihwa Ong and Stephen Collier. Pp. 439–463. Malden: Blackwell.

Ruckenstein, M & Schüll, N. 2017. "The Datafication of Health." *Annual Review of Anthropology.* Vol. 46. Issue: 1, pp. 261 – 278.

Sabucedo, J.-M., Aalzate, M. & Hur, D. 2020. "COVID-19 and the metaphor of war (COVID-19 y la metáfora de la guerra)." *International Journal of Social Psychology.* Vol. 35: pp. 618–624.

Samuel, R. 2021. "Bridging our Digital Divide." [online webpage] Available: https://newhamvoices.co.uk/bridging-our-digital-divide/ [Accessed 20/06/2021].

Samuel, G & Lucivero, F. "Framing ethical issues associated with the UK COVID-19 contact tracing app: exceptionalising and narrowing the public ethics debate." *Ethics Inf Technol*. Vol. 24, Issue: 5.

Stokel-Walker, C. 2021. "The NHS App has Quietly become a Vaccine Passport." In *WIRED magazine*. [online article] Accessed: https://www.wired.co.uk/article/nhs-app-covid-vaccine-passport

Taylor, L. 2020. *There's an app for that: technological solutionism as COVID-19 policy in the Global North*. Tilburg: Tilburg University.

Till, C. 2014. "Exercise as Labour: Quantified Self and the Transformation of Exercise into Labour." *Societies*, Vol. 4; pp. 446–462.

Weissenrieder, M. & Fairclough, N. "Critical Discourse Analysis: The Critical Study of Language." *Mod. Lang*. Vol. 81, Issue: 428.

Whitelaw, S., Mamas, M. A., Topol, E. & van Spall, H. G. C. 2020. "Applications of digital technology in COVID-19 pandemic planning and response." *The Lancet Digital Health*. Vol. 2, pp. 435–440.

Williamson, B. 2015. "Algorithmic skin: health-tracking technologies, personal analytics and the biopedagogies of digitized health and physical education." *Sport Education Society*. Vol. 20, pp. 133–51.

Winnick, D., Jones, M., Cosgrove, P., Murgatroyd, L., Strong, K. 2021. "Vaccine Passports: A Threat to Liberty or a Necessary Safeguard?" [online open letters/article] Available: https://www.theguardian.com/world/2021/feb/25/vaccine-passports-a-threat-to-liberty-or-necessary-safeguard [accessed: 20/05/2022].

Wodak, R. 1989. *Language, power, and ideology: studies in political discourse*. Amsterdam and Philadelphia: J. Benjamins Pub. Co.

Wodak, R. (eds.). 2001. *Methods of Critical Discourse Analysis, Vol. 1*. New York and London: SAGE.

Wodak, R. & Meyer, M. 2009. "Critical Discourse Analysis: History, Agenda, Theory, and Methodology." in *Methods of Critical Discourse Analysis*. New York and London: SAGE.

Young, Robert (ed.). 1981. *Untying the Text: A Post-Structuralist Reader*. Boston, London and Henley: Routledge & Kegan Paul.

Zylinska, J. 2004. "The universal acts" *Cultural Studies*. Vol.18, pp. 523–537.

Pandemic Solutionism
The Power of Big Tech during the COVID-19 Crisis[1]

Felix Maschewski, Anna-Verena Nosthoff

Abstract

In this article, we investigate how Big Tech companies have used the novel coronavirus disease (COVID-19) pandemic to increase their social, political, cal, infrastructural, and epistemic power. We focus on four companies that were outspoken in their efforts to combat the virus: Alphabet (also known as Google), Apple, Facebook, and Amazon (GAFA). During the crisis, these companies evolved as adaptive entities that responded to the state of emergency by promptly rolling out various technological solutions, exemplifying what we call 'pandemic solutionism', that is, the belief in the potential to solve the complex virological crisis of COVID-19 through the integration of digital tools. We identify the activities of GAFA in pandemic solutionism in five key areas that can be defined as the dominant realms of Big Tech's involvement: (1) mapping COVID-19, (2) researching COVID-19, (3) tracing COVID-19, (4) treating COVID-19, and (5) managing COVID-19. In this context, we provide the first comprehensive overview of Big Tech's multifaceted engagement in researching COVID-19 based on wearable technologies, which have been actively promoted as potentially beneficial tools for detecting the coronavirus since the beginning of the crisis. Additionally, through a critical mapping of the multiple activities of selected Big Tech players during the pandemic, it becomes evident how unexpected societal disruptions can lead to the increased dominance by these players. As we demonstrate, Big Tech companies have been able to present themselves as saviours capable of acting more promptly than the state, pushing pandemic solutionism and taking up tasks without being burdened by democratic deliberations. In doing so, they have manifested their infrastructural power, which frequently (such as with contact tracing) establishes the normative framework in which political and social actions take place.

Keywords

Covid-19 pandemic, Big Tech, solutionism, digital capitalism, digital health

---

1   Several passages of this article are based on preliminary, more journalistic research and shorter articles on Big Tech and COVID-19 that we published in the midst of the pandemic in *Jacobin, Republik* and *Philosophie Magazin*: https://jacobin.com/2021/10/big-tech-google-apple-facebook-amazon-health-care-surveillance-capitalism-data; https://www.republik.ch/2020/05/09/wie-big-tech-die-pandemie-loesen-will; https://www.philomag.de/artikel/ausweitung-der-trackingzone. We are grateful for the helpful comments and suggestions by the peer reviewers of this article.

Etymologically, the term 'crisis' is derived from the Greek *krino* and means 'cut', 'select', or 'judge' (cf. Koselleck 2002: 237), and, "by extension, to measure, to quarrel, to fight" (ibid.); it refers to a situation that implies a decisive turning point in a temporary state of uncertainty in which different possibilities are considered. As Reinhart Koselleck writes, the "concept implied strict alternatives that permitted no further revision: success or failure, right or wrong, life or death, and finally, salvation or damnation". Before fanning out into different realms, including psychology, politics, and the economy, the term 'crisis' was particularly characterised by its use in the medical context. Here, it refers to the critical moment where a patient's life is at risk and their fate is decided; thus, the term has a unique time dimension. Against this backdrop, the COVID-19 crisis is a reminder of the original sense of 'crisis'. The early stages of the pandemic required swift medical, economic, and political decisions, while politicians often had to make decisions based on incomplete knowledge given the initial lack of insight into the nature of the virus. Thus, the COVID-crisis was a reminder of the origin of the term 'crisis' both in the sense that political decisions were based on incomplete knowledge and in the way these decisions were existential.

Furthermore, the pandemic has shown how a moment of crisis can create space for a renegotiation of sovereignty. More precisely, COVID-19 has indicated how a reassessment of sovereignty has taken place not only on behalf of governments, but also on that of private technology companies, who, as we show in the following, were involved in several existential decisions from the very beginning of the crisis. Political and private actors were required to promptly and actively respond to the crisis alike. Early on, the public, healthcare officials, and politicians called for digital solutions to better track and map the virus, with ambivalent outcomes (cf. Milan 2020; Whitelaw et al. 2020). In the existing research literature on the topic, both privacy-friendly and totalitarian misuses of tracking technology have been observed throughout of the pandemic (Dix 2020; Cassiano et al. 2021); ethical concerns about tracking technologies and their potential implications for large-scale surveillance have equally been discussed (Bigo 2021; Morely et al. 2022; Newell 2021) alongside discussions surrounding the specific form of governmentality reinforced by tracing apps (Engemann 2020; Bigo et al. 2021). In addition, numerous studies have rightfully focused on authoritarian regimes' misuse of technological tools (Eck et al. 2020, Kitchin 2020). Research on the legitimacy and forms of tracing technologies is beginning to grow, addressing important aspects of how technologies have been harnessed politically in response to the crisis. However, the role of private actors remains understudied. This holds specifically regarding the production of technological 'solutions' that states and authorities relied on (for an initial broad overview, see Lopez Solano et al. 2022; regarding public–private partnerships in Europe during the pandemic, see Storeng et al. 2021).

To address this gap, this article discusses how selected actors have actively contributed to both digital mapping and research practices since the beginning of the COVID-19 pandemic. We chose some of the most powerful companies in the Western landscape and focused on four that have been outspoken in their efforts to beta the virus: Alphabet (also known as Google), Apple, Facebook, and Amazon (GAFA). During the crisis, these companies evolved as adaptive entities that responded to the state of emergency by quickly rolling out diverse technological solutions, culminating in what we call 'pandemic solutionism'. Our analysis shows that—next to the extent and forms of pandemic solutionism—Big Tech's increasing involvement in numerous branches of healthcare reveals both the existential status of these companies and our dependency on their infrastructures, especially during the crisis. Our analysis also outlines the complexity and density of their power in multiple areas of our lives, some of which (including health care) are only beginning to emerge as research topics (see Sharon 2018; Nosthoff & Maschewski 2019; 2022a; Gleiss et al. 2021). Furthermore, existing studies of digital capitalism have hitherto neglected the role that societal crises play in the formation, reproduction, and strengthening of Big Tech's power by focusing on portraying leading actors in digital capitalism as disrupting agents that provoke crises of established industries (as exemplified by the famous motto 'move fast and break things'; cf. Staab 2019; Zuboff 2019; Srnicek 2018).[2] This article attempts to respond to this shortcoming by assessing how unexpected societal disruptions can equally lead to an increase in power of Big Tech actors, using the pandemic as an example.

To shed light on the dynamic surrounding pandemic solutionism, we first explore the most prominent examples and delineate how Big Tech has played a role in responding to COVID-19. We follow critical data studies' views on "the ways in which data are generated, curated, and how they permeate and exert power on all manner of forms of life" (Iliadis & Russo, 2016). Methodologically, we broaden this perspective by investigating the data extracted as well as the actors extracting the data; i.e. the activities of Big Tech in selected realms, a trajectory that we have elsewhere termed 'critical Big Tech studies' (Maschewski & Nosthoff 2022).[3] To this end, identify the activities of the most prominent tech giants—GAFA—in pandemic solutionism in five key areas that emerged from our analysis as the

---

2   To be precise, Srnicek (2018) focuses on the dotcom crash to explain the dominance of Big Tech, yet, analyses that go beyond considering the fragility of financial markets have remained limited.

3   We envision 'Critical Big Tech Studies' as a 'field that studies the political power and political impact of Big Tech as much as a field that critically deconstructs the narratives of Big Tech, that is, their reproduction of AI mythology, etc. What we conceive of as particularly vital is the critical analysis of how they establish private–public partnerships, such as with nation-states, research institutions, health institutions, the educational sector, etc., and thereby strengthen their own infrastructural power. (Maschewski & Nosthoff 2022b)

dominant realms of Big Tech's involvement: (1) *mapping COVID-19*, (2) *researching COVID-19*, (3) *tracing COVID-19*, (4) *treating COVID-19*, and (5) *managing COVID-19*. In this context, we provide the first comprehensive overview of Big Tech's multifaceted engagement in researching COVID-19 based on wearable technology. Focusing on wearables is especially fruitful for our analysis as smart watches have been actively promoted as potentially beneficial tools for detecting the coronavirus early on.

Subsequently, through a critical mapping of the multiple activities of Big Tech players, we analyse how these companies have mobilised the pandemic to increase their social, political, and infrastructural power. Indeed, after numerous scandals and congressional hearings, the pandemic has given these tech giants a chance to present themselves as the leading lights of a new, digitalised healthcare branch. As we argue, the pandemic has also provided these companies ample opportunities to regain credibility for solutionist narratives that were discredited following the so-called 'techlash', which arose in the aftermath of the Cambridge Analytica scandal (Smith 2018). Thus, the cutting-edge products and services that these companies are employing to relaunch their old idealised (self-)image will likely entrench their positions of power within what Shoshana Zuboff has famously termed 'surveillance capitalism' (Zuboff 2019)–a form of capitalism that instrumentalises and exploits user data for the sake of the market and monopolistic power, thereby creating 'asymmetries of knowledge' (Zuboff 2020) and enabling them to colonise even remoter regions.

Before we delve into the activities of Big Tech in detail, we will briefly re-examine a moment of crisis, which, bearing in mind Koselleck's definition, can be seen as having given rise to a 'turning point' at the beginning of the COVID-19 pandemic.

Renegotiating Technological Sovereignty in a Time of Crisis: Pandemic Solutionism

A key moment in which technological sovereignty was renegotiated during the global COVID-19 crisis occurred on April 10, 2020, when Apple and Google announced simultaneously on their websites that there had never been "a more important moment" to "work on solving one of the most urgent problems in the world".[4] The two monopolists announced that they would jointly develop an interface for so-called contact tracing, a technology for tracing coronavirus infections via smartphone based on Bluetooth technology. According to the tech giants' shared promise, "[t]hrough close cooperation and collaboration with developers, governments, and public health providers, [we] hope to harness the power of

---

4   https://covid19.apple.com/contacttracing

technology to help countries around the world".⁵ In other words, engineers from California set out once again to save humanity through technological tools. The solutionist character of the narrative was particularly reflected in the opening sentences of the statement: "Across the world, governments and health authorities are working together to find solutions to the COVID-19 pandemic, to protect people and get society back up and running. Software developers contribute by crafting technical tools to help combat the virus and save lives".⁶

In retrospect, this scene stands out as the epitome of what we term pandemic solutionism, partially drawing on Evgeny Morozov's (2013) much-discussed concept of solutionism. Morozov (2013: 5) defines 'solutionism' as a Silicon Valley-based mindset that recasts 'all complex social situations either as neatly defined problems with definite, computable solutions or as transparent and self-evident processes that can be easily optimized—if only the right algorithms are in place'. On this basis, by 'pandemic solutionism', we refer first to the widespread belief in the possibility of solving the complex virological crisis of COVID-19 through the integration of digital tools alone, or at least in playing a significant role in resolving the crisis through technological means. Second, we allude to the instrumentalisation of the pandemic to accelerate the production of these solutions. It is worthwhile noting that the belief in pandemic solutionism was shared by governments worldwide to varying degrees during the COVID-19 pandemic: Apple's and Alphabet's cooperation on contact-tracing occurred when solutionist promises were not alien to the US, the European Union (EU), and global politics; for instance, the EU promoted 'digital solutions during the pandemic', citing efforts by Facebook and Google (Alphabet) and emphasising their good relations with Big Tech in their shared response to the crisis (cf. European Union 2020). Furthermore, only a few weeks before Apple's and Google's announcement regarding contact tracing, the then-US president made it equally clear that he believed in pandemic solutionism. "I want to thank Google", Donald Trump said at a media conference, thanking the company for having developed a website for comprehensive COVID-19 testing with '1,700 engineers' (New York Times 2020). Trump was referring to a new website developed by Alphabet and its subsidiary Verily (companies, which, as we will elaborate on later, have been at the heart of developing diverse forms of pandemic solutionism). The website, Trump was convinced, "is going to be very quickly done, unlike websites of the past, to determine whether a test is warranted and to facilitate testing at a nearby convenient location" (New York Times 2020). The president was seemingly convinced that Alphabet's endeavours would help everyone, everywhere: "We cover this country and large parts of the world" (ibid.)

For this paper, it is irrelevant that this promise was greatly exaggerated and the website was at best a rough draft, and that the wide availability of testing more wishful thinking than reality at the time. Far more interesting was the attitude of

---

5   Ibid.
6   Ibid.

elected politicians: In the event of a pandemic, the White House trusted (or was evidently dependent) on the tech elite, so much that it seemingly regained belief in its 'solutionist ethic' (Nachtwey & Seidl 2020) after the tech clashes of years past. The situation thus pointed to a huge gap in state sovereignty (cf. Clover 2021), which the Silicon Valley corporations filled determinedly. Moreover, some of the most experienced and powerful technology companies in the Western hemisphere were by no means naive when they entered the stage, as they had been expanding into the healthcare sector for years (cf. Sharon 2018; Nosthoff & Maschewski 2019) after gathering expertise in tracking using smartphones and wearables. Finally, at the height of the first wave of the coronavirus, the decisive moment seemingly arrived for them to assert themselves as pioneers of a data-driven healthcare system while presenting themselves as saviours. Big Tech seemingly followed a well-known motto: *Never let a serious crisis go to waste.*

Alphabet: Mapping, Researching, Tracing, and Managing COVID

To exemplify Big Tech's endeavours during COVID-19 and their myriad forms of pandemic solutionism ranging from *mapping, researching, tracing,* and *treating* to *managing COVID-19*, it is helpful to examine the activities of one of the most determined companies in the industry: Alphabet. Early on, the company pursued numerous initiatives to help combat the spread of the virus, covering almost all of the aforementioned areas, and focusing specifically on managing, treating, mapping and researching COVID-19. While government institutions dithered, the tech giant, in collaboration with its subsidiary Verily, got down to business developing a website, the one that Trump alluded to at a time when the site hardly existed to help US states and regions coordinate testing.[7] In collaboration with local authorities, Alphabet bypassed bureaucratic hurdles to quickly open testing stations. Owing to its own certified testing laboratory, the tech company was able to offer drive-through COVID screenings to the public and establish itself as a beacon of hope on the crisis response map. Since then, it has continued to expand its operations to more towns and cities, offering more than 350 testing sites. While acknowledging several setbacks and concerns about data protection, an internal report from April 2021 claims that the venture has tested nearly 3.9 million people.[8] To participate in the tests, people first need to 'donate' sensitive health data to Alphabet, including information on their history of treatments, illnesses, and the doctors they have consulted in the past. Initially, even a Gmail account was necessary. Verily has also begun studies into immune system responses to

---

7 https://www.projectbaseline.com/studies/covid-19/
8 https://verily.com/2020-impact-report/

COVID-19[9] and the distribution of antibodies[10] among the population by drawing in part upon data from the screenings. More specifically, people who test positive for the virus during the screenings are offered the chance to 'contribute to crucial research' led by a 'dedicated study team'.[11] Verily states that 178,000 participants opted to be part of its 'Baseline COVID-19 Research Programme', which assesses the impact of the pandemic on mental health and wellbeing.[12]

Alphabet's move to join the forces of combating COVID-19 was rather unsurprising to those who have witnessed Big Tech's multifaceted entrance into the healthcare market in recent years. It is helpful to give a short overview of its many projects to understand Alphabet's role in this: Alphabet has invested relentlessly in both start-ups and established companies in the healthcare sector—the most prominent example being Alphabet's acquisition of Fitbit in 2019 (cf. MacCall 2020)—and has conducted research on smart contact lenses and surgical robots. With a venture focused on artificial intelligence (AI) called DeepMind, it has worked to develop algorithms for predicting disease progression to organise bed occupancies in clinics (cf. Powles & Hodson 2017). Additionally, the company recently launched an AI-powered assist tool to identify skin conditions (although the tool contains several problematic biases).[13] To be sure, such AI applications are promising (cf. Davenport et al. 2019). However, they also require an enormous amount of patient data. In recent years, Google has obtained millions of data records on disease progression through partnerships with external healthcare providers, often without patients' knowledge or consent (Pilkington 2019).

In other instances, Alphabet has simply collected patient data itself. Since 2015, Alphabet has even had its own in-house specialist for this kind of data collection alone: Verily (formerly Google Life Sciences), which was instrumental in setting up COVID-testing sites as well, conducts major health studies and even promises to 'redesign the future of health'.[14] To investigate disease development, Verily set up Project Baseline in 2017, a venture for conducting studies (in collaboration with Google) into both individual diseases (such as type-2 diabetes) and the lifestyles of entire age cohorts.[15] For its ongoing Health Study, which began in 2018, the company has provided 10,000 people with so-called 'study Watches' to measure their activity over four years—from the daily number of steps they take to the quality of their sleep.[16] Participants must regularly fill out surveys and submit them to clinical check-ups and tests, ranging from eye tests to blood samples, thus

---

9 https://www.projectbaseline.com/studies/covid-immune-response/
10 https://www.projectbaseline.com/studies/covid-research/
11 Ibid.
12 Cf. https://verily.com/2020-impact-report/
13 https://blog.google/technology/health/ai-dermatology-preview-io-2021/
14 https://www.projectbaseline.com/shape-healthtech/
15 https://www.projectbaseline.com/
16 https://www.projectbaseline.com/studies/project-baseline/

offering the company a panoptic glimpse into countless aspects of their lives. As Project Baseline's website states, after having mapped the world through Google maps, the aim is to 'map human health'.[17]

A few years ago, companies had to enter into expensive partnerships with healthcare providers to gain access to valuable patient data. Owing to Google and Verily, Alphabet is coming to resemble a healthcare provider. At the same time, it is not only using its infrastructure, cloud services, AI, and datasets to conduct research, but is also growing its own business. Verily has expanded relentlessly in precision medicine, extending its corporate network and operating device-supported platforms (such as Onduo) that offer personalised, algorithmic health management through digital phenotyping and telemedicine applications.[18] In 2021, Verily even entered the insurance market through 'Granular Insurance',[19] thus joining the broader trend toward personalised, digitised insurance models (cf. McFall et al. 2018).

Throughout the pandemic, Verily launched Healthy at Work, a programme for companies and institutions to continuously screen their workforce for COVID-19; they even recently assessed the programme's effects on workforce health in an in-house study (cf. Poole et al. 2021). Thus, in addition to having emerged as a provider in COVID-19 early on by offering mapping and tracing technology and services, Alphabet engages in building tools for *managing COVID-19*. Healthy at Work operates as follows: Using an app, employees fill out a daily symptom survey, and on the grounds of predictive modelling, employers can monitor their health. Using cloud infrastructure, Verily also provides testing kits and polymerase chain reaction (PCR) testing, and can track both vaccine compliance and booster shots. Recently, it has been conducting 50,000 tests per week and has administered three million tests in total.[20] Since its launch in late 2020, the programme now has over 150,000 participating employees, including 20 clients such as the University of Alabama and Waymo, a self-driving car company.[21]

In addition to Verily's health mapping, Alphabet also engages in traditional mapping modes with its Google Health Division (a subsidiary of Alphabet dedicated to health services) and Google Maps, which is used to produce Google's COVID-19 Community Mobility Reports.[22] These reports have been utilised by numerous local authorities worldwide. Published every few days, they provide information about population movement trends by drawing on aggregated and anonymised location data from smartphone users, data that are normally used to show how busy certain locations (such as bars, cafés, and parks) are at different

---

17 https://www.projectbaseline.com/
18 https://onduo.com/
19 https://granularinsurance.com/who-we-are/
20 https://verily.com/2020-impact-report/
21 https://verily.com/2020-impact-report/
22 https://www.google.com/covid19/mobility/

times of day. This illustrates how convenient services from the company can be turned into administrative tools, lending credibility to the necessity of their general tracking endeavours. A similar project offered by Google Health is the COVID-19 Open Data Repository, an easy-to-access collection of COVID-19-related information, that intends to "help public health professionals, researchers, policymakers, and others gain insight into the virus".[23] While the maps charted by Alphabet might appear as a helpful service to the average user, they are also a means of legitimising data accumulation by surveillance capitalists while enabling them to capture new territory in an exploratory fashion.

However, Alphabet and the GAFA companies more generally have not been content to simply analyse movement patterns; they also investigate ways to detect COVID-19 as early as possible. To this end, the summer of 2020 saw several studies developed around the sensory capacities of fitness trackers and smartwatches, exemplifying how several Big Tech actors are now also active in *researching COVID-19*. For several of these studies, users of wearable devices could become 'citizen scientists' by donating personal data, from their daily physical activity to their sleep cycles. Wearable-based studies on COVID-19 have remarkably that it is difficult to keep track of them, fuelling hopes that smart gadgets can be useful in fighting COVID-19 and other pandemics in the future (Amft et al. 2020).

It is worthwhile to review several of these studies to understand the extent of Big Tech's involvement in research and the breadth of their collaboration with research institutions worldwide. For instance, since acquiring Fitbit, Alphabet has cooperated with Scripps Research Institute in the context of the so-called 'Detect' study (Quer et al. 2021). The circle of participants is made as broad as possible. Any self-tracker who lives in the US can take part through various wearables (such as Apple Watch and Fitbit) and upload their bodily data directly via the MyData-Helps app. Symptoms are 'detected' early on, and individual data are 're-socialised' so that sources of infection can be recorded on maps and localised more precisely. A similar initiative was launched in Germany by the Roland-Koch-Institute (cf. Urban 2022), a German federal agency and a leading research institute responsible for disease control and prevention, where self-trackers can donate their data in the context of the Corona-Datenspende-App.[24] In this context, almost 550,000 users have donated their data as of July 2022.[25]

It is worth noting that 'Detect' is a remake of a previous study published in January 2020, which examined what is known as real-time flu tracking in approximately 200,000 Fitbit wearers; the study was conducted at a time when Fitbit had not yet been acquired by Alphabet (cf. Radin et al. 2020). Data on resting heart

---

23 https://health.google/covid-19/
24 https://www.rki.de/DE/Content/InfAZ/N/Neuartiges_Coronavirus/Corona-Datenspende.html
25 https://corona-datenspende.de/science/ (last accessed July 14th, 2022)

rate and sleep were recorded via the fitness bracelet, using which (according to the results of the Detect study) far more precise prognoses of influenza could be made than with conventional means. The tracking was not entirely objective though. The sleep data were not truly accurate, nor was it always possible to clearly distinguish between the more severe pulse associated with flu and that of everyday stress. However, the authors of the Detect study point to the great potential of wearable technology, which, with its increased distribution, should soon make more comprehensive, timelier monitoring possible. (ibid.)

It is precisely this potential (alluded to by its predecessor study) that the 'Detect' study attempts to translate into reality. Hence, biometric variables (such as daily activity) are being used to expand the depth of surveillance. In addition to the 'Detect' study, Fitbit launched an in-house study, which, in a similar vein, assessed the possibility of wearable devices to identify potential COVID-19 symptoms early on (Natarajan et al. 2020). However, the reliance on wearables is precarious; it may result in a social pressure to adapt to the technology by users, citizens, and workers, as well as lead to algorithmic biases that can disadvantage marginalised groups (Colvonen et al., 2020).

Apple: Researching and Tracing COVID-19

In addition to Alphabet and its subsidiary Verily, another company is active in the realm of health tech research and focuses on COVID-19: Apple. As such, it is no surprise that one of the most prominent wearable-based COVID-19 studies was dedicated exclusively to the Apple Watch. In the 'Warrior Watch Study'[26] conducted through cooperation between eight New York City hospitals (specifically the Mount Sinai Health System), researchers discovered that the Apple Watch could detect possible signs of COVID-19 infection, that is, minimal changes in heart rate variability occur up to seven days before symptoms emerge (cf. Hirten et al. 2021).

While not exclusively focused on the Apple Watch, renowned medical research institutes, including Scripps Research and Stanford University, have performed similar studies on personal sensor data such as physical activity, resting heart rate, sleep, or even skin temperature (cf. Mishra et al. 2020; Alayj et al. 2021). Likewise, early on in the pandemic, the Zuckerberg San Francisco General Hospital began to investigate how wearable technologies could compensate for a lack of comprehensive tests (cf. Smarr et al. 2020). The 'Oura-Ring'—that measures both heart rate and breathing rate during sleep—diagnoses coronavirus infections even before symptoms arise. Hospital employees, who are at risk from constant contact with infected people, were equipped with the smart, tight-fitting device, resulting in interesting data. The aim of real-time tracking was initially to allow hospital

---

26 https://www.mountsinai.org/about/covid19/warrior-watch-study

employees to act more quickly so that ailing employees could potentially be identified, checked, and treated in a more targeted manner.

Regarding Apple, researchers from the Seattle Flu Study and the University of Washington recently launched the 'Apple Respiratory Study',[27] a collaboration with Apple, to grasp the extent to which the Apple Watch 6 could predict respiratory illnesses such as COVID-19, particularly examining heart rate and oxygen levels in the blood. While such studies may appear to have stemmed from the COVID-19 crisis, they have had a long history of prevalence in Silicon Valley. For example, since 2019, Apple Watch users have been able to harness the company's proprietary Research app to donate their health data to a selected number of universities, hospitals, and institutions (such as the World Health Organization [WHO]) to support new scientific discoveries or the development of innovative products. This feature followed a broader trend. For example, in the Apple Heart Study, which was carried out as early as 2017 to 2018, more than 400,000 Apple Watch users had already contributed their data in cooperation with Stanford Medicine to analyse atrial fibrillation (Perez et al. 2019). This exemplifies how the narrative has shifted in recent years, with Apple rebranding itself as a company investing in global health care and the future of health, Apple Watch being the most iconic symbol of this transition. The wearable, indeed, is no longer presented as a device helping to optimise one's activity; instead, it seeks to optimise health, not just of individuals but of humanity overall (cf. Maschewski & Nosthoff 2019, 2022). Wearables have emerged as tools for societal tracking, pointing to the normalisation of tracking devices throughout society, fuelled by insurance models (cf. Mau 2019) and so-called 'wellness programmes' in companies.[28] Exposing one's intimate data is not seen as a flaw, but as part of the consumer experience and a more altruistic project in which donating individual data leads to a greater goal, recalling Zurawski's (2021: 92) observation that surveillance, in general, is increasingly coming to resemble a 'feature'; hence Apple's promotional claim that "the future of health research is you".[29] In line with this declaration, Apple CEO Tim Cook announced, as early as 2019, that if one were to look back at Apple's business in a few years, its greatest contribution would have been 'about health' (Gurdus 2019).

In addition to being active in *researching* COVID-19 with diverse partners and based on their wearable technologies, Apple, next to Alphabet, has also played a significant role in *tracing COVID-19*. For those following Apple's and Google's health research in recent years, their April 2020 decision to work together on COVID-19 contact tracing hardly came as a surprise.[30] As already alluded to in

---

27 https://seattleflu.org/appleresipratorystudy
28 https://community.virginpulse.com/
29 https://www.apple.com/ios/research-app/
30 https://www.apple.com/newsroom/2020/04/apple-and-google-partner-on-covid-19-contact-tracing-technology/

the beginning, claiming that there was never "a more important moment to work together to solve one of the world's most pressing problems" by harnessing the power of technology, these tech companies did not wish to wait for government actors to create a contact tracing app based on their standards. Instead, in a technocratic and metapolitical fashion, they presented their own 'comprehensive solution': a proprietarily developed interface for enabling decentralised, anonymised data exchange via Bluetooth that now forms the basis for almost all national tracing apps. To be sure, this decentralised app, which is rooted in open source, is favourable to centrist models enabling state surveillance on a large scale. However, the fact that these companies—understood here as 'para-state agents' (Vogl 2021: 104)—created such a rigid, virtually inescapable standard underscores the source of their authority: their infrastructural power. Procedurally, and from the standpoint of democratic legitimacy, Apple's and Alphabet's decision and their dictate on the type of app that could be used at all was emblematic of a decision that was non-negotiable by nation-states, thus revealing Big Tech's *political* power (cf. Sharon 2020).

Facebook: Mapping COVID

As a third party that helped combat the pandemic, it is useful to consider Facebook, which has been particularly active in *mapping COVID-19*. Facebook developed a COVID-19 information centre for the Newsfeed to combat anti-vax fake news. Facebook's efforts in this realm were explicitly encouraged and promoted by the EU, quoting Facebook's activities, next to efforts by Google to 'launch new tools' to counter false information (cf. EU 2020). In addition to developing a smartwatch that will feature various health tools, the social network has targeted users with surveys to help researchers from Carnegie Mellon University and the University of Maryland produce a weekly 'Interactive Map' of self-reported symptoms for tracking the virus.[31] Every day, more than 50,000 people complete these surveys by providing information about their age and place of residence, and answering questions about whether they are experiencing symptoms (such as cough or fever), as well as feelings of anxiety or depression. Facebook does not receive the data from these surveys, thereby appearing as a rather neutral, altruistic actor here.

However, Facebook does not always play the role of an uninvolved medium. In line with the narrative of pandemic solutionism outlined earlier (which views complex epidemiological problems as being easily resolvable through the provision of additional data), the platform has expanded its proprietary Disease Prevention Maps, which early on played a role in promoting the narrative of pandemic solutionism.[32] Facebook's mapping project constitutes a different attempt at improving

---

31   https://dataforgood.facebook.com/covid-survey/?region=WORLD
32   https://dataforgood.fb.com/tools/disease-prevention-maps/

'the effectiveness of health campaigns and epidemic response'[33] and was put into place as early as 2019 to track cholera in Mozambique. With newly developed tools such as 'colocation maps', 'movement maps', and 'network coverage maps', the company is recording how its users' movement radii and social contacts contribute to the spread of the virus, and whether existing lockdown measures are effective or need to be modified.[34] Meanwhile, the project's motto of 'Data for Good' sounds like a familiar solutionist promise.[35]

Facebook's CEO Mark Zuckerberg has treated the crisis as an opportunity to transform Facebook from a 'social' network into a collaborative research network. This is exemplified by his donation of $25 million to the research hub COVID-19 Therapeutics Accelerator, as well as by an ongoing networking effort that culminated in the launch of the COVID-19 Mobility Data Network. In this context, Facebook has managed to forge partnerships with leading universities globally, such as the Harvard School of Public Health and Princeton University, extending their network as far as the Bill & Melinda Gates Foundation. This 'nonpharmaceutical intervention'[36] aims to use real-time data provided by apps such as Facebook Messenger to track the spread of the virus more accurately and create predictive models to forecast the course of the crisis.

In the past, such data were chiefly used to identify user preferences, predict consumer behaviour, and target users with ads based on their movement (cf. Zuboff 2019). However, just as with Google's Mobility Reports, the surveillance-capitalist zeal for data collection is now being recast in an altruistic light. In Zuckerberg's words, which embody the narrative of pandemic solutionism reproduced by Silicon Valley actors throughout the COVID-19 pandemic, "The world has faced pandemics before, but this time we have a new superpower: the ability to gather and share data for good".[37] Evidence that Facebook's movement pattern maps have been helpful during the crisis remains largely absent. Notwithstanding, in February 2021, it began offering health organisations and governments up to $120 million worth of free ad space to promote initiatives such as vaccination campaigns.[38] The company is thus sparing neither expense nor effort to win over the public with its systems update. That said, in view of the recurring data leaks occurring at the same time (cf. Holmes 2021), it is plausible that the company has attempted to 'health-wash' its image.

33   Ibid.
34   https://dataforgood.fb.com/docs/covid19/
35   https://dataforgood.fb.com/
36   https://visualization.covid19mobility.org/?date=2021-03-24&dates=2020-12-24_2021-03-24&region=WORLD
37   https://www.washingtonpost.com/opinions/2020/04/20/how-data-can-aid-fight-against-covid-19/
38   https://about.fb.com/news/2021/02/reaching-billions-of-people-with-covid-19-vaccine-information/

Amazon: Researching, Managing, and Treating COVID

Another well-known company has emerged at the intersection of health and tech during the pandemic: Amazon. While it is less research-oriented than business-like, it has begun to make a name for itself in digital well-being. Amazon's interventions at times fall more implicitly under the category of *managing, treating, and researching COVID-19*, but they are substantial nevertheless for understanding the power shifts surrounding COVID-19 and the various dimensions of 'biosurveillance' (Reichert 2018) that have emerged from it. Moreover, the company is explicitly active in treating COVID-19. During the pandemic, the world's self-proclaimed 'most customer-centric company' launched an entire line of new projects designed to have far-reaching effects. After acquiring the online pharmacy PillPack as early as 2018, in late 2020, Amazon announced further plans for Amazon Pharmacy, a service for prescription medications.[39] Establishing itself in this sector—which is already valued at $900 billion US dollars (cf. Neumann et al. 2020)—appears to be part of a long-term strategy that is continuously taking shape. Also, Amazon's cloud service, Amazon Web Services (AWS), has supported the biotechnology company AbCellera, which discovered two antibody treatments for COVID-19.[40]

Amazon established the telemedicine platform Amazon Care, a service that offers comprehensive medical care on a 24/7 basis.[41] Through messaging or video chat, employees throughout the US can receive diagnostic advice from doctors on COVID-19, as well as on any other illness. Additionally, members can receive a COVID-19 test. Patients are able to schedule house calls or arrange for medical care at their workplace. The stated goal is to make medical treatment smoother, more immediate, and more efficient by making waiting rooms and pharmacy visits superfluous and to develop more "customer-centric ways for patients to get the health care services, products, and medications they need" (Landi 2021). The company therefore effectively responds to patients' needs to be treated remotely in a time of 'social distancing', thus preparing for potential future pandemics. This round-the-clock monitoring is being sold by the company as part of a new therapy model, which it is pitching as "healthcare built around you".

In addition to Amazon Care, the company introduced a fitness tracker in the summer of 2020, called Amazon Halo, to compete with market leaders such as Apple Watch and Google's Fitbit.[42] This device can also be used by users to participate in studies tracking the coronavirus; it employs AI built for new dimensions of health analysis. Halo includes features such as the measurement of steps,

---

39 https://pharmacy.amazon.com/
40 https://aws.amazon.com/de/blogs/industries/finding-enduring-solutions-to-the-evolving-covid-19-crisis/
41 https://amazon.care/
42 https://www.amazon.com/Amazon-Halo-Fitness-And-Health-Band/dp/B07QK955LS

heart rate, and skin temperature. Moreover, it offers a type of 3D scan to provide a body-fat analysis twice as accurate as leading at-home smart scales: Users need to upload photos of their naked selves into the Amazon cloud, which are used to generate simulations of their body, thereby promising to deliver a 'more complete picture' of their health.[43] Commentators assessed the device as "the most invasive tech we've ever tested", noting the voice-recording feature that harnesses 'affective computing' to draw conclusions about the emotional state of its wearers and how they are perceived by others (cf. Fowler et al. 2020). User emotions, allegedly detectable from the voice (from happiness to frustration) are being recorded and analysed in real time, ostensibly to improve wearers' mental well-being and intersubjective communication.

Amazon has already assembled broad knowledge of its customers' preferences and consumption habits and knows when people are at home (cf. West 2019). During the COVID-19 crisis, however, the company expanded its surveillance to the body and mind. Pursuing a threefold intervention (Amazon Pharmacy, Amazon Care, and Amazon Halo), it constructed an all-encompassing digital health system and a comprehensive ecosystem in which diverse aspects of life were permeated with surveillance-capitalist tools. The extent of their efforts is, last but not least, reflected in Amazon's AWS Diagnostic Development Initiative launched in 2020, a "20 [million dollar] commitment to accelerate research and innovation to advance the collective understanding and detection of COVID-19 and other infectious diseases in order to mitigate current and future outbreaks".[44]

Big Tech Becoming "Environmentalitarian" During COVID-19

This article's overview of the endeavours of four of the largest Western technology companies illuminates how GAFA have long ceased functioning as mere businesses. Instead, they have become tightly woven infrastructures that gather data on our online behaviours, preferences, and traits, information on which we physically depend ever more profoundly, as evident by their entry into the healthcare sector. Against this backdrop, the pandemic has prompted transformations that were already in motion, causing them to be aggressively pursued by tech companies seeking to expand their operations. Regarding their many activities in health tech, and specifically in combating COVID-19 (ranging from *tracing COVID-19, mapping COVID-19, and managing COVID-19* to *researching* and *treating COVID-19*) in collaboration with subsidiaries, research networks, and on the basis of wearable technologies, these companies are reinventing themselves as cartographers of the body. Moreover, they have arisen as adaptive entities

---

43   https://www.youtube.com/watch?v=qohYemzkGgo
44   https://aws.amazon.com/de/government-education/nonprofits/disaster-response/diagnostic-dev-initiative/

and tight-woven ecosystems that have been highly responsive to the situational demands of the pandemic, instrumentalising the uncertainty of the situation and the lack of a clear political strategy at their ends (cf. Du et al. 2022).

GAFA companies have not only benefited immensely from the increased social dependency on digital infrastructures throughout the pandemic—from online meetings to online education (cf. Klein 2020)—they have also been instrumentalising the crisis to become active agents that shape how countries react to it, thereby laying the groundwork for playing an even greater role in similarly precarious circumstances in a potentially pandemic-struck future. They do so by assembling sensitive healthcare data that only they have access to and that only they can leverage when needed, thereby cultivating a monopoly on data knowledge and extending their position as 'data-driven intellectual monopolies' (Rikap and Lundvall 2020) in the realm of health. This results in a two-fold epistemic asymmetry: First, the involvement of GAFA gives rise to, as Stefania Milan (2020) argues in a more general context, the epistemic question of "which 'other' nonstandard ways of knowing and being in the world in [terms of] infrastructure, dynamics and governance" are neglected at the expense of datafied and proprietary forms of knowledge produced by Western Big Tech companies (and their implicit rationales) to 'solve' the crisis. Second, it is crucial to mention that the platform companies themselves will be able to dictate the conditions of cooperation with research institutes now and in the future, and will control access to proprietary data, algorithms, and knowledge, culminating in epistemic power. As Shoshana Zuboff (2019, 11) remarks: "Surveillance capitalism operates through unprecedented asymmetries in knowledge and the power that accrues to [become] knowledge. Surveillance capitalists know everything *about us*, whereas their operations are designed to be unknowable *to us*. They accumulate vast domains of new knowledge *from us*, but not *for us*".

As a consequence, the interventions of Big Tech go way beyond simply managing the effects of the current crisis. Instead, at certain points, Big Tech decided *politically on* which infrastructure societies and states needed to rely on to handle the pandemic, implicitly focusing on potential future crises as well. Indeed, several technology oligopolies not only built the tools to help politics combat the pandemic; they also played an active role as nonrepresentative, non-elected political agents deciding on matters of public concern, thus lending credence to recent research that has portrayed Big Tech actors not only as economical, but as prominently political actors (cf. Seemann 2021; Vogl 2021; Srivastava 2021). As seen from our critical mapping of tech giants' numerous activities, their practices allow them to expand their business operations and revenue streams, or to develop services that virtually they alone can provide due to their financial resources and data reserves. Furthermore, they use their practices to subtly extend their power and give rise to what could be termed 'Big Health Tech': the expansion of monopolist data extractivism into healthcare (cf. Nosthoff & Maschewski 2022a).

Ultimately, the crisis has widened the field of possibility for Big Tech companies to practice and experiment with what we have elsewhere and more generally described as 'surveillance-capitalist biopolitics' (Nosthoff & Maschewski 2022a), a form of data extraction aiming to govern both the individual body and the body politic. Such a form of biopolitical governance is no longer limited to a governance of bodies mediated by the state in a classical Foucauldian sense. Instead, private actors now increasingly define health standards and deviations from the norm, as exemplified by the myriad projects of Alphabet's Verily. Surveillance-capitalist biopolitics can hence be defined as a culmination of cybernetic control techniques and capitalist market mechanisms that constantly enables and requires new forms of individual behavioural adaptation, leading to unequal exposure to surveillance and targeting. These forms of adaptation rely on datafied regulatory measures of the body; that is, the feedback-based mediation of correlated, biometric target values. They channel their effectiveness less often through static regulations and transparent norms and more so through fluid, personalized transcripts that operate in real time and on the grounds of proprietary algorithms (cf. ibid.). It is important to note that surveillance-capitalist biopolitics often leads to a platform-economic, epistemic asymmetry that manifests in companies' ability to develop products and services exclusively and monopolistically, and to control access to bodily knowledge. Such biopolitics is usually entirely or partially privatized in public-private partnerships (ibid.). In this process, as Erich Hörl (2021) aptly points out with reference to Foucault's concept of "environmentality", the medium (in this case, mostly wearable tech) itself becomes increasingly "environmentalitarian" (2021: 122). This could equally be said of technology companies themselves. As such, Big Tech and the media they develop are part of a "new apparatus of capture [...] whose principle is the capture and control of reality itself." (Hörl 2021: 109) Thus, by delivering the structures of our communication as well as our bodily existence (given their multifaceted expansion into healthcare) in a time of 'social distancing', they increasingly form the sine qua non of our reality, providing the digital conditions of possibility for crisis response(s) and subsequently benefiting from renegotiations of sovereignty in moments of uncertainty.

Although a promotional video for Verily's Project Baseline calls on viewers to "make your mark on the map of human health",[45] this might be seen as more accurately describing the behaviour of tech giants. Indeed, as political scientist Will Davies (2018: 186) describes the logic of platformisation in relation to GAFA, "the ultimate objective of Internet companies [...] is to provide the infrastructure through which humans encounter the world. [...] When the mind wants to know something, it will go to Google; when it wants to communicate with someone, it will turn to Facebook. When we want to be somewhere else, we click on Uber, and when we simply want something, Amazon will make it arrive". A similar logic can

---

45 https://www.youtube.com/watch?v=FQSSovdC7fY

now be observed in health care and health research, where Big Tech excessively invests in providing new digital infrastructure. Dominance in this respect could, as discussed in the article, already be seen during COVID-19 in a different context. Indeed, Apple's and Alphabet's cooperation to provide the binding infrastructure for many COVID-19-tracing apps has shown their infrastructural power and at times the non-negotiability of their political choices.

During the COVID-19 crisis, tech companies have been able to present themselves as saviours that can act more quickly than the state, pushing pandemic solutionism and taking up tasks without being burdened by the processes of democratic deliberation. In doing so, they have manifested their infrastructural power, which frequently (such as with contact tracing) establishes the normative framework in which political and social actions take place. At the same time, they have continued to deepen their probing of everyday life and the individual and social body while selling the public digital colonisation (or 'data colonialism' as Nick Couldry and Ulises Mejias [2019] term it) and surveillance-capitalist biopolitics (cf. Nosthoff & Maschewski 2022), disseminating solutionist narratives that have been reproduced in politics.

Developments that appear understandable or necessary during a pandemic can quickly take on a life of their own. From GAFA's solutionist standpoint, no amount of data collection will ever be enough. Lack of adequate regulations will prompt such companies to use opportunities to acquire more data about the world and us. Hence, the increasing involvement of tech actors in health care and health research calls for critical mapping that outlines their extending spheres of influence alongside the meticulous legal monitoring of their activities on behalf of regulatory bodies, as well as the critical assessment of their solutionist narratives, especially in a time of prolonged crisis. Given the developments outlined in this paper, it is imperative to not forget that 'crisis'—stemming from *krinein*, as Koselleck (1973: 196f.) reminds us—also etymologically implies 'critique'.

References

Alavi A./Bogu, G. K./Wang, M., et al. (2022): "Real-time alerting system for COVID-19 and other stress events using wearable data." *Nature Medicine* 28, pp. 175–184.
Amft, O./González, L. I. L./Lukowicz, P., et al. (2020): "Wearables to fight COVID-19: From symptom tracking to contact tracing." *IEEE Pervasive Computing* 19(4), pp. 53–60.
Bigo, D. (2021): *Pandemic Surveillance*. London: Polity.
Bigo, D./Guild, E./Kuskonmaz, E.M., et al. (2021): "Obedience in Times of Covid-19 pandemics: a renewed governmentality of unease?" *Global Discourse* 11(3), pp. 471–489.

Cassiano, M. S./Haggerty, K./Bernot, A. (2021): "China's Response to the COVID-19 Pandemic: Surveillance and Autonomy." *Surveillance & Society* 19(1), pp. 94–97.

Clover, J. (2021): "The rise and fall of biopolitics: a response to Bruno Latour." *Critical Inquiry* 47(S2), pp. 28–32.

Colvonen, P.J./DeYoung, P.N. /Bosompra, N.O.A., et al. (2020): "Limiting racial disparities and bias for wearable devices in health science research." *Sleep* 43(10), pp.1–3.

Couldry, N./Mejias U.A. (2019): "Data Colonialism: Rethinking Big Data's Relation to the Contemporary Subject." *Television & New Media* 20(4), pp. 336–349.

Davenport T./Kalakota R. (2019): "The potential for artificial intelligence in healthcare." *Future Healthcare Journal* 6(2), pp. 94–98.

Davies, W. (2018): *Nervous states: How feeling took over the world*. London: Random House.

Dix, A. (2020): "Die deutsche Corona Warn-App – ein gelungenes Beispiel für Privacy by Design?" *Datenschutz und Datensicherheit – DuD* 44, pp. 779–785.

Du, J./Xu, J./Zeng, X., et al. (2022): "Amazon's Strategic Shift in the Face of the COVID-19." In: *Advances in Economics, Business and Management Research 656, Proceedings of the 2022 2nd International Conference on Enterprise Management and Economic Development (ICEMED 2022)*, pp. 1019–1028.

Eck, K./Hatz, S. (2020): "State surveillance and the COVID-19 crisis." *Journal of Human Rights* 19(5), pp. 603–612.

Engemann, C. (2020): "Pandemic Media: On the Governmediality of Corona Apps." In: Philipp Dominik Keidl et al. (eds.): *Pandemic Media: Preliminary Notes toward an Inventory*. Lüneburg: meson press, pp. 185–193.

European Commission (2020): "Digital Solutions during the Pandemic." Available online: https://ec.europa.eu/info/live-work-travel-eu/coronavirus-response/digital-solutions-during-pandemic_en.

Fowler, G. A./ Kelly, H. (2022): "Amazon's new health band is the most invasive technology we've ever tested." *Washington Post,* December 10. Available online: https://www.washingtonpost.com/technology/2020/12/10/amazon-halo-band-review/.

Gleiss, A./Kohlhagen, M./Pousttchi, K. (2021): "An apple a day – how the platform economy impacts value creation in the healthcare market." *Electron Markets* 31, pp. 849–876.

Gurdus, L. (2019): "Tim Cook: Apple's greatest contribution will be 'about health'." *CNBC.com,* January 8. Available online: https://www.cnbc.com/2019/01/08/tim-cook-teases-new-apple-services-tied-to-health-care.html.

Hirten, R. P./Danielletto M./Tomalin, L., et al. (2021): "Use of Physiological Data From a Wearable Device to Identify SARS-CoV-2 Infection and Symptoms and Predict COVID-19 Diagnosis: Observational Study." *J Med Internet Res* 23(2):e26107.

Holmes, A. (2021): "533 million Facebook users' phone numbers and personal data have been leaked online." *Business Insider,* April 3. Available online: https://www.businessinsider.com/stolen-data-of-533-million-facebook-users-leaked-online-2021-4?r=DE&IR=T.

Hörl, E. (2021): "Critique of Environmentality. On the Worldwide Axiomatics of Environmentalitarian Time." In: Erich Hörl, Nelly Y. Pinkrah, Lotte Warnsholdt (eds.), *Critique and the Digital.* Berlin: Diaphanes, pp. 109–145.

Iliadis, A./Russo, F. (2016): "Critical data studies: An introduction." *Big Data & Society* 3(2), https://doi.org/10.1177/2053951716674238.

Kitchin, R. (2020): "Civil liberties or public health, or civil liberties and public health? Using surveillance technologies to tackle the spread of COVID-19." *Space and Polity* 24(3), pp. 362–381.

Klein, N. (2020): "How big tech plans to profit from the pandemic." *The Guardian (The Intercept),* May 13. Available online: https://www.theguardian.com/news/2020/may/13/naomi-klein-how-big-tech-plans-to-profit-from-coronavirus-pandemic.

Koselleck, R. (1973): *Kritik und Krise. Eine Studie zur Pathogenese der bürgerlichen Welt.* Frankfurt a.M.: Suhrkamp.

Koselleck, R. (2002): *The Practice of Conceptual History. Timing, History, Spacing Concepts.* Stanford: Stanford University Press.

Landi, H. (2021): "Amazon taps former Prime executive to oversee virtual care, pharmacy and diagnostics businesses", *Fierce Healthcare,* December 19. Available online: https://www.fiercehealthcare.com/tech/amazon-taps-former-prime-executive-to-oversee-virtual-care-pharmacy-and-diagnostics-businesses.

Lopez Solano, J./Martin, A./Ohai, F., et al.(2022): "Digital Disruption or Crisis Capitalism? Technology, Power and the Pandemic. A Report by the Global Data Justice Project",, *Tilburg Institute for Law, Technology and Society.* Available online: https://globaldatajustice.org/wp-content/uploads/2022/05/Global-Data-Justice-Digital-disruption-or-crisis-capitalism-03-2022.pdf.

Maschewski, F./Nosthoff, A.V. (2019): *Die Gesellschaft der Wearables. Digitale Verführung und soziale Kontrolle.* Berlin: Nicolai.

Maschewski, F./Nosthoff, A.V. (2022a): "Überwachungskapitalistische Biopolitik: Big Tech und die Regierung der Körper." *Zeitschrift für Politikwissenschaft* 32, pp. 429–455.

Maschewski, F./Nosthoff, A.V. (2022b): "Big Tech and the Smartification of Agriculture." In: IT for Change (ed.), *State of Big Tech 2022, Dismantling Digital Enclosures.* Available online: https://projects.itforchange.net/state-of-big-tech/big-tech-and-the-smartification-of-agriculture-a-critical-perspective/.

Mau, S. (2019): *The Metric Society: On the Quantification of the Social.* Cambridge: Polity.

McCall, B. (2020): "15 ways Silicon Valley is harnessing Big Data for health." *Nature Medicine* 26, pp. 7–10.

McFall, L./Meyers, G./Hoyweghen, I. V. (2020): "The personalization of insurance: Data, behaviour and innovation." *Big Data & Society* 7(2), https://doi.org/10.1177/2053951720973707.

Milan, S. (2020): "Techno-solutionism and the standard human in the making of the COVID-19 pandemic." *Big Data and Society* 7(2), https://doi.org/10.1177/2053951720966781.

Mishra, T./ Wang, M./ Metwally, A.A., et al. (2020): "Presymptomatic detection of COVID-19 from smartwatch data." *Nature Biomedical Engineering* 4, pp 1208–1220.

Morley, J./Cowls, J./Taddeo, M., et al. (2020): "Ethical guidelines for COVID-19 tracing apps, Protect privacy, equality and fairness in digital contact tracing with these key questions." *Nature* 582, Comment, pp. 29–31.

Morozov, E. (2013): *To Save Everything, Click Here. The Folly of technological Solutionism*. New York: Public Affairs.

Nachtwey, O./Seidl, T. (2017): " Die Ethik der Solution und der Geist des digitalen Kapitalismus." *IfS Working Paper* #11, Institut für Sozialforschung, Frankfurt/M. Available online: http://www.ifs.uni-frankfurt.de/wp-content/uploads/IfS-WP-11.pdf.

Natarajan, A./Su, H.W./Heneghan, C. (2020): "Assessment of physiological signs associated with COVID-19 measured using wearable devices." *npj Digit. Med.* 3, 156. https://doi.org/10.1038/s41746-020-00363-7.

Neumann, K./Kleipaß, U./Rong, O., et al. (2020): "Future of Health. Der Aufstieg der Gesundheitsplattformen." Available online: https://www.rolandberger.com/de/Insights/Publications/Future-of-Health-Der-Aufstieg-der-Gesundheitsplattformen.html.

Newell, B. (2021): "Introduction: Surveillance and the COVID-19 Pandemic: Views from Around the World." *Surveillance & Society* 19(1), pp. 81–84.

Newlands, G./Lutz, C./Tamò-Larrieux, A., et al. (2020): "Innovation under pressure: Implications for data privacy during the Covid-19 pandemic." *Big Data & Society* 7(2), https://doi.org/10.1177/2053951720976680.

New York Times (2020): "Transcript: Trump's Coronavirus News Conference." March 13. Available online: https://www.nytimes.com/2020/03/13/us/politics/trump-coronavirus-news-conference.html.

Perez, M. V./Mahaffey, K.W./Hedlin, H., et al. (2019): "Large-scale assessment of a Smartwatch to identify atrial fibrillation." *New England Journal of Medicine* 381(20), pp. 1909–1917.

Pilkington, E. (2019): "Google's secret cache of medical data includes names and full details of millions." The Guardian, November 12. Available online: https://www.theguardian.com/technology/2019/nov/12/google-medical-data-project-nightingale-secret-transfer-us-health-information.

Poole, S.F./Gronsbell, J./Winter, D., et al. (2021): "A holistic approach for suppression of COVID-19 spread in workplaces and universities." *PLOS ONE* 16(8):e0254798.

Powles, J./Hodson, H. (2017): "Google DeepMind and healthcare in an age of algorithms." *Health and Technology* 7, pp. 351–367.

Quer, G./Radin, J.M./Gadaleta, M., et al. (2021): "Wearable sensor data and self-reported symptoms for COVID-19 detection." *Nature Medicine* 27, pp. 73–77.

Radin, J. M./Wineinger, N. E./Topol, E.J., et al. (2020): "Harnessing wearable device data to improve state-level real-time surveillance of influenza-like illness in the USA: a population-based study." *The Lancet Digital Health*, 2(2), pp. 85–93.

Reichert, R. (2018): "Biosurveillance, Self-Tracking und digitale Gouvernementalität." In: Buhr, L./Hammer, S./Schölzel, H. (eds.) *Staat, Internet und digitale Gouvernementalität. Staat – Souveränität – Nation.* Springer VS: Wiesbaden, pp. 65–86.

Rikap, C./Lundvall, B.-Å. (2022): "Big tech, knowledge predation and the implications for development." *Innovation and Development* 12(3), pp. 389–416.

Seemann, M. (2021): *Die Macht der Plattformen: Politik in Zeiten der Internetgiganten.* Berlin: Ch. Links Verlag.

Sharon, T. (2018): "When digital health meets digital capitalism, how many common goods are at stake?" *Big Data & Society* 5(2), https://doi.org/10.1177/2053951718819032.

Sharon, T. (2021): "Blind-sided by privacy? Digital contact tracing, the Apple/Google API and big tech's newfound role as global health policy makers." *Ethics and Information Technology* 23(S1), pp. 45–57. DOI: 10.1007/s10676-020-09547-x.

Smarr, B.L./Aschbacher, K./Fisher, S.M., et al. (2020): "Feasibility of continuous fever monitoring using wearable devices." *Scientific Reports* 10, 21640, https://doi.org/10.1038/s41598-020-78355-6.

Smith, E. (2018): "The techlash against Amazon, Facebook and Google—and what they can do." *The Economist*, January 20. Available online: https://go.nature.com/2K41ZAA.

Srivastava, S. (2021): "Algorithmic Governance and the International Politics of Big Tech.", *Perspectives on Politics*, pp. 1–12. doi:10.1017/S1537592721003145.

Srnicek, N. (2017): *Platform Capitalism.* London: Polity Press.

Staab, P. (2019): *Digitaler Kapitalismus.* Berlin: Suhrkamp.

Storeng, K.T./de Bengy Puyvallée, A. (2021): "The Smartphone Pandemic: How Big Tech and public health authorities partner in the digital response to Covid-19". *Global Public Health* 16(8-9), pp. 1482–1498.

Urban, M. (2022): "'Toll. Ich bin froh dabei zu sein'". Studie zur Spende digitaler Körperdaten in der Corona-Krise." *ZQF–Zeitschrift für Qualitative Forschung* 22(2), pp. 9–10.

Vogl, J. (2021): *Kapital und Ressentiment. Eine kurze Theorie der Gegenwart.* Munich: C.H. Beck.

Wen, H./Zhao, Q./Lin, Z., et al (2020): "A study of the privacy of covid-19 contact tracing apps." In: Park, N./ Sun, K./ Foresti, S., et al. (eds): *Security and Privacy in Communication Networks. SecureComm 2020. Lecture Notes of the Institute for Computer Sciences, Social Informatics and Telecommunications Engineering*, vol 335. Springer, Cham. https://doi.org/10.1007/978-3-030-63086-7_17.

West, E. (2019): "Amazon: Surveillance as a service." *Surveillance & Society* 17(1/2), pp. 27–33.

Whitelaw, S./Mamas, M. A./Topol, E., et al. (2020): "Applications of digital technology in COVID-19 pandemic planning and response." *The Lancet Digital Health* 2(8), pp. 435–440.

Zuboff, S. (2018): *Das Zeitalter des Überwachungskapitalismus*. Frankfurt am Main/New York: Campus.

Zuboff, S. (2020): "Caveat User: Surveillance Capitalism as Epistemic Inequality." In: Kevin Werbach (ed.), *After the Digital Tornado*. Cambridge University Press: Cambridge, pp. 174–214.

Zurawski, N. (2021): *Überwachen und Konsumieren. Kontrolle, Normen und soziale Beziehungen in der digitalen Gesellschaft*. Bielefeld: transcript.

Staging Science Policy:
Storytelling in the Public

Introducing Science through Images
Visual Knowledge Communication on SARS and Covid-19

Christopher Frieß, Ramón Reichert

Abstract

On close examination of visual material used by various national and international health authorities during public representation and communication regarding Covid-19, especially its virus particles, it can be observed that among other things, image processing methods and strategies such as reinterpretation or recycling of archived material are used in the utilization of viral image material.

The example of the US-American Centre for Disease Control and Prevention (CDC) will be used to illustrate the ease with which images are used, processed, and recycled, even in a scientific context. Our interest concerns a transmission electron microscope image published already in 1975 by Dr. Fred Murphy and Sylvia Whitfield. (Fig. 1) It shows virus particles (virions) from the human coronavirus 229E, as currently designated by the CDC. This image has been labelled in many cases as SARS-CoV-2 and has been used and published by institutions, authorities, as well as through media in various degrees of image processing in the form of multiple variations.

To approximate the changes that Murphy and Whitfield's image underwent, we use snapshots saved in the digital archive Wayback Machine[1] to reconstruct chronologies of the material's development.

From our analysis, we conclude that modes of representation in the scientific context shape the conditions of knowledge production. The popular image of the virus connects to pictorial traditions, serves an educational purpose and by its nature has an immediate impact on the viewer. While we consider the popularisation of knowledge to be inherent to the scientific field, popularising interventions on microscopic images lead to an increase in visual appeal which may ultimately have shaped the scientific field itself.

Keywords

Covid-19 pandemic, science communication, virus representation, popularisation, history of science

---

1   Wayback Machine is operated as part of the non-profit project Internet Archive. (URL: https://web.archive.org)

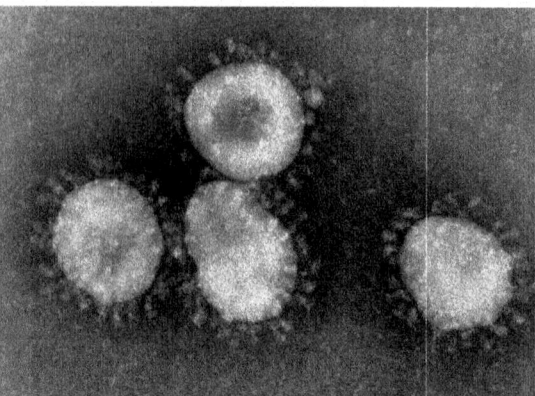

Fig. 1: Murphy et al., 'TEM image of Human coronavirus 229E. PHIL ID#10270', 1975, source: phil.cdc.gov

Visual Practices of Science Communication

Scientific images shape the knowledge processes of the scientific community, their visual representations enable new insights, create the framework of international knowledge communication, and influence the securing of evidence in scientific research. (Mitchell 2015) The reproduction of an observation using electronic or digital devices, instruments and imaging media, technologies and infrastructures is integrated into complex procedures of knowledge construction. (Hentschel 2014) As mechanical, objective, and neutral as scientific images may be, their evidentiary power is always due to a specific aesthetics, their ability to be told and a rhetoric of scientific nature. (Bredekamp/Dünkel/Schneider 2019) As a result, in a scientific context of use, visualisations are tied into a historical period and are imbued with specific styles, arguments, and illustrations. In this sense, scientific images that are embedded in the use of specific media of recording, storage, and data processing and that circulate within certain research collectives can always be viewed as scientific constructs that are subject to a certain pictorial logic.

Images of medical research are used in different contexts of production and reception of scientific knowledge. (Brennen/Simon/Nielsen 2021:277–299) In the image laboratories, which is the narrower field of scientific research and development, they are involved in processes of recording, storing, processing, authenticating, and disseminating data, information, and knowledge; in an expanded field of knowledge communication in heterogenous cultural spaces, their image-producing production and mediation processes always also include popular cultural shifts in meaning:

"We routinely engage with images of the pandemic, whether through epidemiological maps or infographics, photographs of masking and physical distancing—or the lack thereof—and the ubiquitous medical illustration of the severe acute respiratory syndrome coronavirus 2 (SARS-CoV-2). These images serve to inform, provide meaning, and illustrate the outbreak narrative in ways that help us process, reflect on, and understand our experiences. The dynamic nature of our engagement with these images allows us to generate collective knowledge about the pandemic in a cultural space where images are created, contested, embraced, and at times transformed into icons." (Callender 2020: 1061–1063)

But the reciprocal conditional relationship between science and science communication can no longer be analytically separated in a meaningful way. Because every order of knowledge develops modes of representation that include both the conditions for the emergence of new knowledge and the conditions for its validity. They not only give scientific knowledge 'additional' stability, normativity, and legitimacy, but can also create a dynamic that significantly influences the constructiveness and contextuality of knowledge production.

The concept of knowledge popularisation does not describe a field of practice that would be outside of 'pure' science, but rather the fact that popularising procedures and rules are inherent in the genesis of scientific knowledge. This point of view criticizes the one-sided assumption that popularisation occurs when 'standardised' specialist knowledge is passed on to a 'passively receptive' lay public by 'homogeneous' research groups. In contrast, our investigation of the image processing of the SARS and CoV-2 virus draws attention to the knowledge-generating aspects of popular knowledge and provides evidence that popularising interventions of microscopic images lead to an increase of visual appeal and thus introduce dramatizing and narrative elements of gaze guidance that elevate attention. In our contribution we try to prove that the different image processing techniques of the technically produced image led to a significant transformation of scientific knowledge, which, however, is difficult for the public to understand, namely that the general public does not understand how the transformation of "knowledge" about viruses has come about. A lay audience takes for granted that coronaviruses can have a colour. (Nguyen/Catalan-Matamoros 2020: 323–328)

The assumption that scientific knowledge is 'primary' knowledge that precedes its exploitative popularisation asserts a 'pure' and 'unadulterated' genesis of knowledge. We would like to elaborate the assumption that scientific visualisations are also always involved in processes of their representative illustration, which can be interpreted as a gesture of visual conviction. A narrow perspective that excludes media, narrative, theatrical, popular, or popularising conditions as formative processes of knowledge tries to hermetically isolate 'pure' knowledge, but ultimately prevents a differentiated investigation of scientific knowledge production. Because our analysis assumes that popularising effects genuinely shape the scientific field itself.

Virion Properties and the Imaging Process

Before analysing the visual material, a brief description will be given of the process used to produce microscopic images of the virus and also an explanation of a major misconception about the property of colour assigned to virions.

It can be stated that the colouring of virions is an arbitrary act, which is based on interpretation and which pursues goals, the fulfilment of which is to be accelerated with the strategies of communication design.

Virions are too small for colour to be assigned to them. In principle, colour itself is not a property of solid entities but an information that our visual system extracts from light, (Webster 1996: 587–588) which is an electromagnetic wave itself. Thus, visible light and its colour can be described by its wavelength. Visible light differentiates itself from other electromagnetic waves by the limitations of the human eye to only be able to see a certain spectrum of wavelengths. (Waldman 2002: 17)

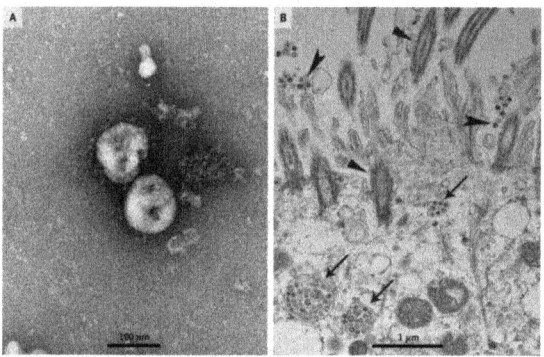

Fig. 2: Zhu et al., 'Visualisation of SARS-CoV-2 using a transmission electron microscope (negative staining)', 2020, source: The New England journal of medicine

Nothing has a colour by itself, since there needs to be light for colour to be perceivable. In order for a human being to see colour, light reflected from an object must impinge on the retina in order to trigger the colour receptors in the form of a visual stimulus. (Rogers 2011) The physiologist Johannes Müller described the relationship between human perception and light with the following words: "[...] without the organ of sight, there would be no light, colour, nor darkness, but merely a corresponding presence or absence of oscillations of the imponderable matter of light."[2] (1840: 261)

---

2   The original text is in German and this quote was printed in the translation of the book: Müller, J. (1842): "Elements of physiology" translated by William Baly

The light visible to humans is in the range of wavelengths between about 360 nm and 830 nm, (Sliney 2016: 226) which can vary slightly depending on age. (Zuclich *et al.* 2005: [no pagination]) A single SARS-CoV-2 virion has a diameter between 60 nm and 140 nm, (Zhu *et al.* 2020: 730) which means that it is too small for the wavelengths of light to be reflected on the virions body and therefore also no colour stimulus can happen.

Microscopic imaging of virions is accomplished using electron microscopy (EM). The image by Dr. Fred Murphy and Sylvia Whitfield was produced using a transmission electron microscope (TEM). In the TEM process, the specimen is dehydrated, cast in resin and cut into ultrathin pieces as part of the preparation process to achieve the smallest possible thickness. (Roingeard et al. 2019: 3) TEM images show a cross-section through the specimen. The imaging process takes place in a vacuum, with the specimen being penetrated by an accelerated electron beam. (Bradbury et al. 2022) The generated image results from the interaction of the electron beam with the specimen. A binary image (contrast image) is formed, which is composed of regions with electrons that have penetrated the specimen and regions without electrons where the specimen could not be penetrated. (Williams/Carter 2009: 373–374) The observed material is, of course, no longer alive.

For the visualisation of virions with the help of TEM, the so-called negative staining method is commonly used. In this process, the specimen is treated with a heavy metal salt solution in the course of its preparation, whereby the heavy metal remains suspended in cavities and at the edges of the specimen. As a result, the virions on the image later appear brighter than their immediate surroundings. (Ludwig-Maximilians-Universität München [no date]; Mayer/Spiess 1976: 4–5) With this knowledge, it is also relatively easy to recognize inverted image material as such.

To draw the conclusion that by inverting, an image is obtained, which gains significance or corresponds to a higher actuality, is to be questioned. Even more, the assignment of colours should be examined with a critical eye. Both the colourised TEM images and any other form of visualisation of SARS-CoV-2 viruses, which might be characterized by colour attribution, are preceded by clear design decisions.

Analysis of Different Image Variations

In the Public Health Image Library (PHIL) of the CDC,[3] the image of Murphy and Whitfield is archived in two versions, both in the form of a neutral black and white image (Fig. 1) and a colourised version (Fig. 3) with virions painted in red and blue surroundings.

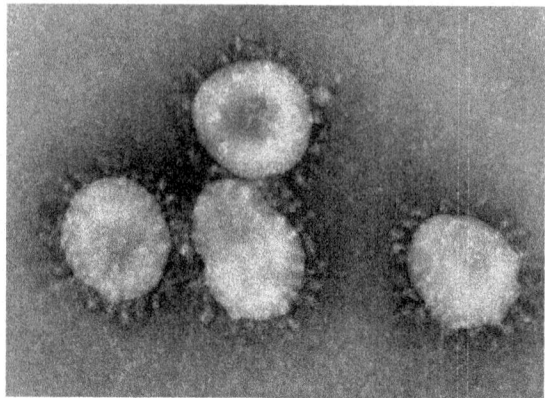

Fig. 3: Murphy et al., 'TEM image of Human coronavirus 229E. PHIL ID#15523', 1975, source: phil.cdc.gov

Looking at snapshots stored in the archive of the Wayback Machine, it can be determined that these images were exchanged between May 14, 2020 (Murphy et al. 2020a) (images corresponding to Fig. 4 or Fig. 5) and October 18, 2020 (Murphy et al. 2020b) (images corresponding to Fig. 1 and Fig. 3). The new version of the black and white image[4] was inverted and rotated. Assuming the other way around that the older version of the image is inverted, considering the characteristics of a negative stained TEM, the current version is possibly the original.

The images in the PHIL are clearly labelled with a unique identification number (ID#). However, the ID was not updated when the images were exchanged with their inverted 'twin', but was simply left as it was, suggesting that the CDC identifies the exact same data as being held in both images.

---

3   According to a reference on the CDC's website (CDC 2022), the images presented in the PHIL are historical archival material and should not be considered a source for the most current matters regarding public health.

4   The corresponding black and white image served as the starting point for the colourised image at a certain point in time.

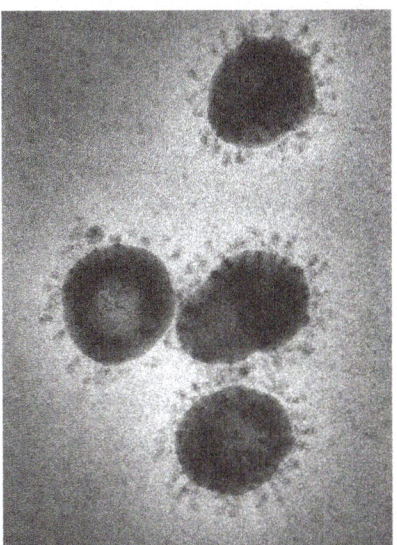 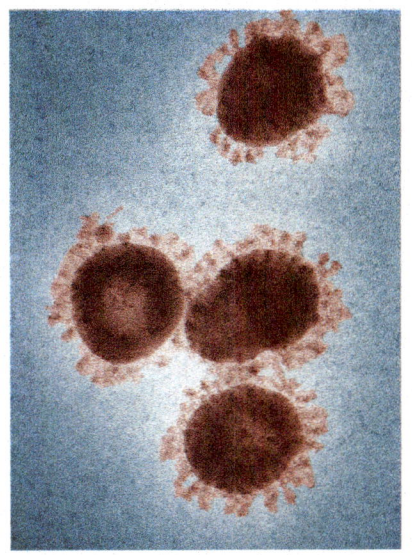

Fig. 4: Murphy et al., 'TEM image showing infectious bronchitis virus (IBV) virions. PHIL ID#15523', 1975, source: phil.cdc.gov

Fig. 5: Murphy et al., 'TEM image showing infectious bronchitis virus (IBV) virions. PHIL ID#10270', 1975, source: phil.cdc.gov

The images in the database are always accompanied by a corresponding text. Both the black and white image (ID#10270) and the colour image (ID#15523) always feature the same description. However, in the course of the image exchange (between May and October 2020), this text and, simultaneously, the definition of the virions were also changed.[5] Whereas previously the virions were attributed to the infectious bronchitis virus (IBV), meanwhile known as avian coronavirus, from October 2020 onwards the same image has been labelled as human coronavirus 229E, without any reference to the reinterpretation and without any explanation for this decision. (Murphy et al. 2020a–b)

The avian coronavirus infects poultry (cases are known to occur in chickens, turkeys, pheasants, and guinea fowls) and belongs to the genus Gammacoronavirus. (de Wit/Cook 2020: 313–314) Human coronavirus 229 E, on the other hand, as the name suggests, affects humans and belongs to the genus Alphacoronavirus. SARS-CoV-2, for which the image has been frequently used and recycled, belongs to the genus Betacoronavirus.

Mammalian coronaviruses belong to the genera Alpha- and Betacoronavirus, while avian coronaviruses mainly belong to the genera Gamma- and Deltacoro-

---

5   Between 2017 and May 2020, the interpretation of the TEM image apparently remained the same, according to archived material. (Murphy et al. 1975a; Murphy et al. 2020a)

navirus. (Nakagawa et al. 2016: 168) There is clear evidence for the reassortment of viruses among different bird species and of viruses recombined between mammals, but the combination of Alpha- or Betacoronaviruses with a Gammacoronavirus is not proven and highly unlikely. Both viruses would have to be present in the same host, in a single cell, at the same time, which is rather difficult to imagine. After all, both viruses cannot replicate in the same host. (de Wit/Cook 2020: 315) Hence, these are two very different categories, considering its either low or severe impact on human health.

Equally noteworthy are the changes that have taken place in the CDC's SARS info section. This section was created in the wake of the 2003 SARS epidemic. In the following, a page with the name 'SARS-CoV Images' (Fig. 6), from the subcategory 'Laboratory Testing and Specimens' will be examined more closely. (CDC 2020c) Here, the focus lies again on the image of Murphy and Whitfield. In this case, the published version (Fig. 7) differs greatly from the other images. Not only have severe colour changes been made[6], but the image material is also lacking in quality and is only available in low resolution. There is not much left of the original image information. But before going into more detail, a brief overview of the development of the website over time will be given. As of December 6, 2017, there is a notice on the website stating that this page has been archived for historical purposes and will not be maintained or updated. (CDC 2017a) Nevertheless, similar to the case in the PHIL, a reinterpretation of the visual material took place here, again without explanation or notice.

In the past, two dates at the bottom of the page provided information about when the content was last modified and when it was last reviewed.[7] Between December 8, 2018 and April 24, 2019, the information regarding the last change of content was removed and from then on only the date of the last review could be read ('Page last reviewed'). (CDC 2018; CDC 2019) This could probably be understood as a logical response to the definition of the website's content as archival material, which has been noted above the content since 2017. After all, archival material is no longer being updated, at least not in the sense of changing the content, and certainly not without reference to such a change. However, there was a content update between October 30, 2020 and November 1, 2020, which, without comment or clarification, is a relatively drastic intervention. After all, it should not be ignored that this is a scientific context. On the website, the date of the last review was adjusted indeed, but there was no comment on the reinterpretation of the image and thus a change in the content. (CDC 2017b; CDC 2020b)

The change relates to the same reinterpretation of the virions as was done in the PHIL. Here, too, the virions were attributed to the human coronavirus 229E instead of the formerly associated IBV. (Murphy et al. 1975a–d) As a result, this

---

6   The virions are painted in ultramarine and the surroundings were colourised in gold ochre.
7   'Page last reviewed' and 'Page last updated'

image version with its blue-coloured virions even went through a total of three different stages of interpretation.

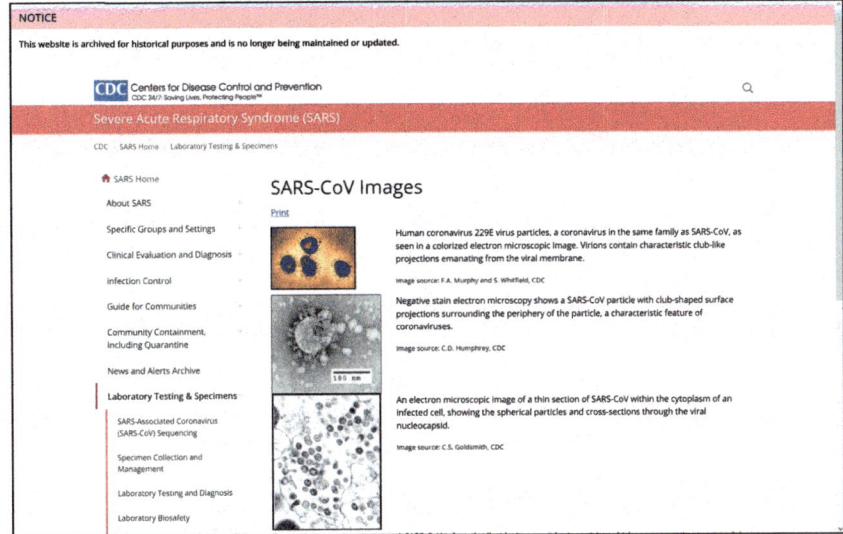

Fig. 6: CDC, 'SARS-CoV Images', 2020, source: cdc.gov/sars/lab/images.html (Screenshot from October 21, 2022)

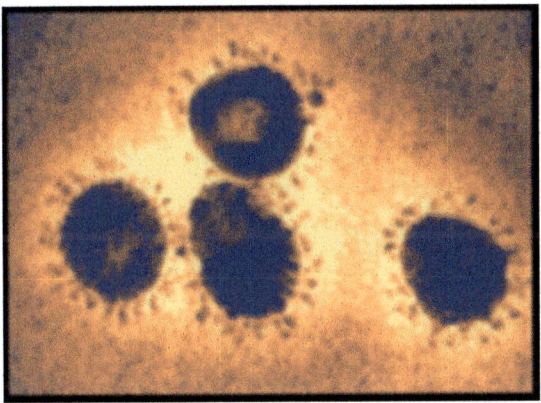

Fig. 7: CDC, 'Human coronavirus 229E virus particles', 2005, source: cdc.gov/sars/lab/images.html[8]

---

8   This colourised image has been used over time as a general icon for SARS (without caption), as representation for infectious bronchitis virus (IBV) virions, and by now depicts the human coronavirus 229E.

Originally, the image was published without accompanying text and served as a general representation of SARS virions. (Fig. 9) (CDC 2005) As of December 6, 2017, the image has been labelled. Hand in hand with the labelling of the image in the PHIL, the virions were assigned to the IBV here as well. (CDC 2017a) Finally, as of October 30, 2020, the assignment of virions to human coronavirus 229E was reinterpreted (Fig. 8). This also occurred shortly after the same changes were made to the images in the PHIL. The image itself, however, remained unchanged since 2005

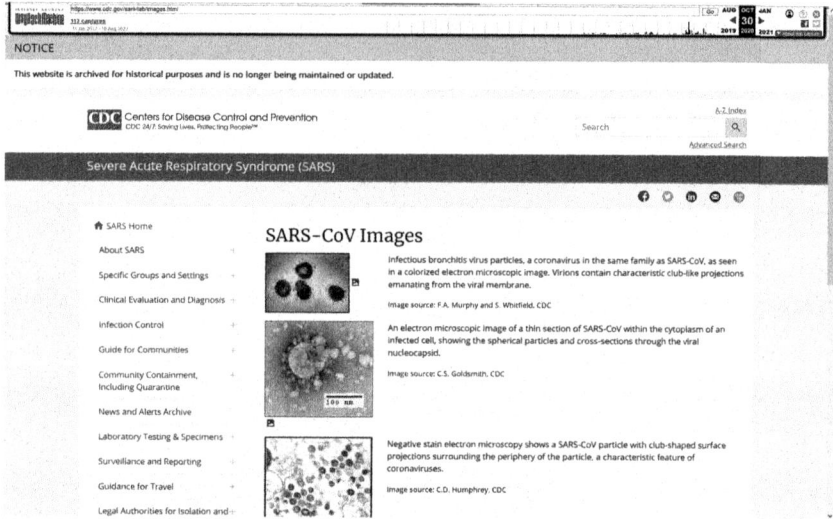

Fig. 8: CDC, 'SARS-CoV Images', 2017, source: cdc.gov/sars/lab/images.html (Screenshot of a snapshot from October 30, 2020 with Wayback Machine)

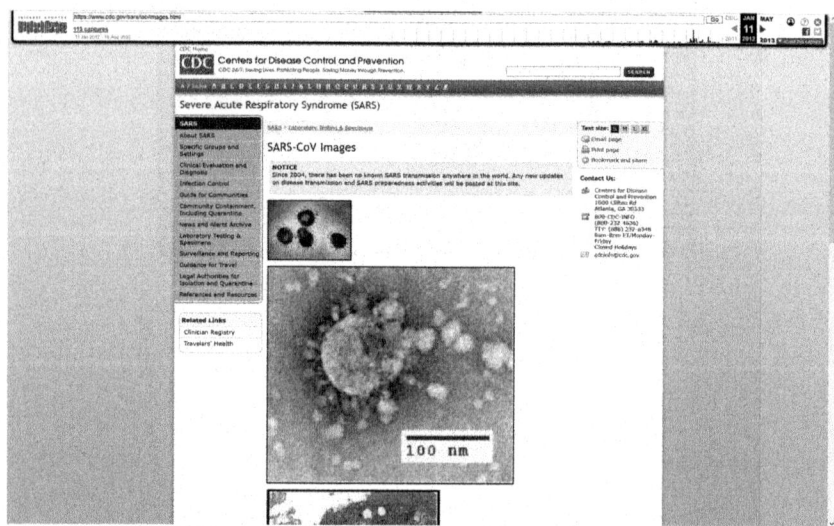

Fig. 9: CDC, 'SARS-CoV Images', 2012, source: cdc.gov/sars/lab/images.html (Screenshot of a snapshot from January 11, 2012 with Wayback Machine)

Advanced Virion Design

Probably the best-known visualisation related to SARS-CoV-2 is the so-called 'spiky blob' a virus visualisation generated with the help of 3D programs (Fig. 10). The ominous-looking virion was designed by medical illustrators Alissa Eckert and Dan Higgins, on behalf of the CDC. According to an interview in the Wallpaper* magazine that Alissa Eckert gave to Alice Rawsthorn, Co-founder of the Instagram Live series *Design Emergency*, the brief included the creation of an identity for the virus, so to say, "a mugshot, something that represents what this enemy is." (Eckert 2020)[9]. According to the requirements of the CDC, the representation of the virus was exaggerated, with the formulated goal of raising the public's awareness about SARS-CoV-2. (Rawsthorn 2020: 174) In order to achieve the design goals, even the shape of the virions was adjusted by changing the number of individual proteins. While the M-proteins[10] were greatly reduced, the focus of the illustration is on the S-proteins[11]. The closed-up depiction and the red colouring were intended to portray the virus dramatically and make it appear threatening.

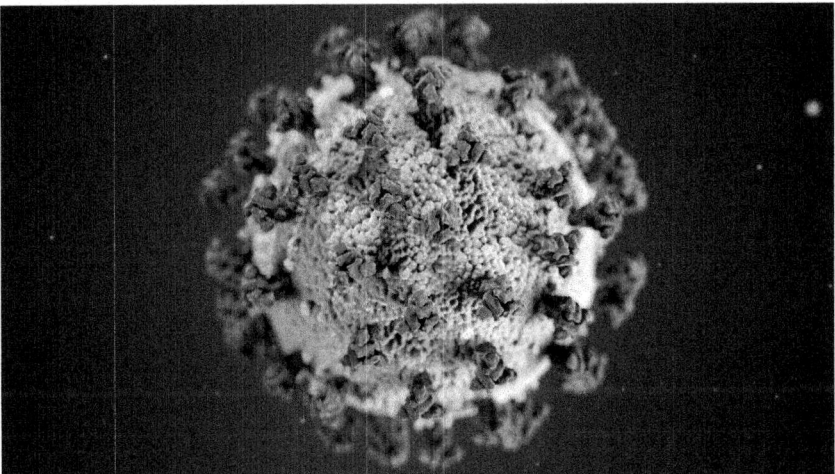

Fig. 10: Alissa Eckert and Dan Higgins, 'spiky blob' 2020, source: phil.cdc.gov

From Eckert's reasoning, it can be concluded that the aesthetics of hyperrealism were purposefully used to make the virions look serious. The idea was to create an image that would help to show people that the virus really existed. For Eckert, it was important that the virion looked as if it could be touched. (ibid.) The designers succeeded quite well in doing so thanks to the use of texture and with the help of theatrical lighting.

9   Alissa Eckert interviewed by Alice Rawsthorn
10   The M-proteins, which stands for Membrane proteins, are shown in orange.
11   The S-proteins, which stands for Spike proteins, are shown in red.

The CDC is probably also very proud of this illustration, after all, the image has already graced the homepage of the PHIL since February 2020. (CDC 2020a)

It can be observed that some renderings of this virus representation use photography related stylistic elements such as blur or a vignette (Fig. 10). Possibly this is to underline their authenticity once again. After all, photography is considered authentic, objective and usually the first choice for documenting visual events or impressions. Moreover, photography can stand for objective reporting, even if not always rightly so. The vignette, in addition to creating associations, also helps to direct the eye specifically to the centre of the image and thus to the virion. It dramatises and supports the depiction of the virus as a hovering threat. The orange dots in the surrounding area are reminiscent of rising fire particles and locate the virion in an apocalyptic-looking environment.

Processed Images for Covid-19 Communication

Images created with the aid of electron microscopes are often published as colourised or even inverted versions in addition to the original. In principle, these manipulated images should ideally be marked as 'colourised' or 'inverted' in the caption, thus avoiding misinterpretation. This is especially important when the images leave the scientific context. Unfortunately, this is not necessarily always implemented accordingly, not even by recognized institutions.

Any colour attribution or inversion directly affects the image's message. Not only does colour trigger various associations in the viewer, but the colourisation of an EM image also results in the loss of image information. Finally, in the presented cases, not even the relative brightness corresponds to the original anymore. In some cases, images were even inverted and published without any indication of their processed, nature leaving the viewer in ignorance.

It may make sense to make use of the mentioned image processing methods in order to emphasize certain areas and thereby work out particularly important details, or in order to direct the focus of the viewer to the essential. Apart from the reasons or interests behind the image processing, the partial manipulation of TEM images in particular is not at all compatible with the original production process of the images, since an electron microscopy image is characterized precisely and solely by its differences in brightness. In the context of a causal chain, when journalists are dependent on the correct information of a scientific source and the readers of a medium are dependent on the precision of journalists and editors, it can easily go unnoticed that in fact some of the images shown are manipulated representation. Especially in digital media, images are often used merely as icons or gap-fillers. The presence of a source is not always given and the use of image captions is usually a rarity.

In many cases, a provider of stock images also joins the causal chain. In order for third parties to be able to sell the rights to use an image such as that of Murphy and Whitfield, the image must of course be modified in some way. After all, the original is provided by the CDC as public domain.[12] As a result, the image of Murphy and Whitfield is now available in a wide variety of colourisations, and these variations have accordingly been published in a wide variety of media, as well as in online presences of institutions and organisations. Even the World Health Organization (WHO) shows a strongly alienated version of the picture of Murphy and Whitfield on an information page on the topic of the COVID-19 vaccination (Fig. 11). The image is shown without any caption or explanation as a so-called 'hero image'.[13] It was originally made available by the contributor Callista Images on the website of the US-American picture agency Getty Images, with the aim of selling the rights of use for a stiff price (Fig. 12).

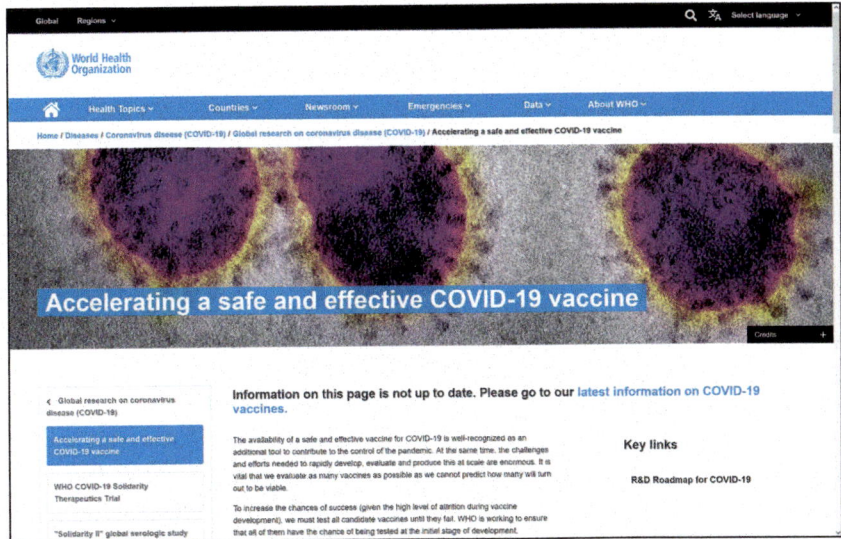

Fig. 11: WHO, 'Accelerating a safe and effective COVID-19 vaccine', 2020, source: who.int (Screenshot from October 22, 2022)[14]

The contributors on these platforms even go one step further and use complex image manipulation methods based on algorithms to create stylization effects in order to alienate the image material. The new image no longer has much to do with the original, and yet it rejoins the mass of circulating versions. One such image, for example, which looks as if it had been edited in Microsoft Word with the help of the 'Artistic Effects' function, even made it into the scientific journal Nature in an article on SARS-CoV-2. (cf. Mallapaty 2020: 19) Originally, the image (Fig. 13) was

---

12 The request to refer to the original source has of course been ignored by the contributors of stock image platforms in this case as well.
13 A 'hero image' is a large web banner at the top of the page.
14 This version of Murphy and Whitfield's image was strongly edited with bright colours and cropped to another proportion.

provided by AMI Images and published on the website of the stock image agency Science Photo Library. At this point, especially when comparing this version with the original from 1975, the arbitrary use of so-called 'creative' filters or other aesthetic choices in connection with scientific images should perhaps be questioned.[15]

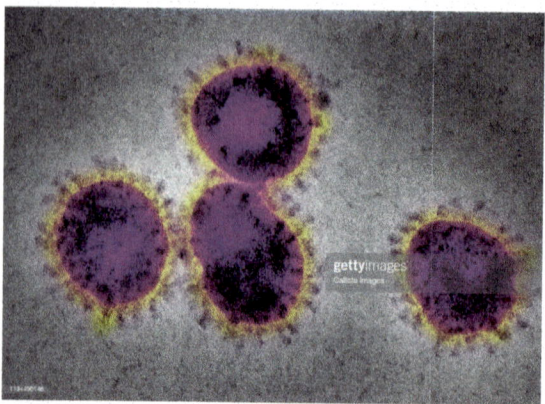

Fig. 12: Callista Images, 'EM Coronavirus, causing SARS - stock photo', n.d., source: gettyimages.com (Accessed: October 22, 2022)[16]

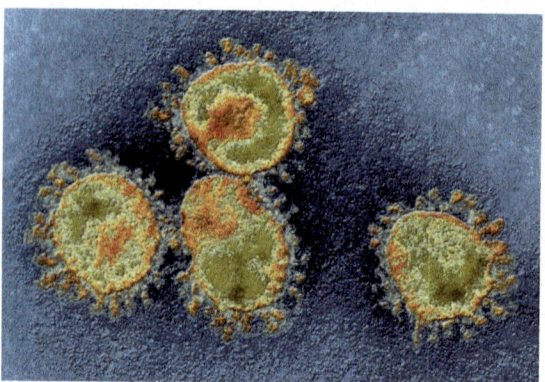

Fig. 13: AMI Images Library/Science Photo Library, '"Human coronavirus, TEM', n.d., source: sciencephoto.com (Accessed: October 22, 2022)[17]

15   The aspect of creativity here may be limited merely to the selection of a stylization filter. It is unclear whether the colours were reassigned here or whether an already processed version of the image served as the starting point.
16   Here, the virions are painted in magenta and surrounded by a yellow corona. The background remained unchanged in greyscale.
17   Strongly modified version of the TEM image by Murphy and Whitfield as published in an article in Nature. In this image, the virions were colourised yellow and orange,

In the following, at least three more cases will be mentioned, which are no longer related to the picture of Murphy and Whitfield, but which also illustrate very well the effects of the causal chain as just described.

The first case deals with an image originally published on the Flickr page of the US National Institute of Allergy and Infectious Diseases (NIAID) research centre. It depicts a TEM image of SARS-CoV-2 virions, which are painted red, with yellow outlines. The spike proteins are shown in turquoise, and the surrounding area is black and blue-green. (NIAID 2020b) The NIAID does not provide a black and white image on the Flickr page, but it does provide the same image with different colours as an alternative, which looks even more menacing due to the usage of intense reds and yellows. (NIAID 2020a)

The first version, as just described, was also shown in an article by Heather Murphy, which appeared in The New York Times on May 26, 2020 (Fig. 14). (Murphy 2020) In the image caption[18], the arbitrarily assigned colours were used as characteristics to describe the virions, without reference to the image processing and possibly in unawareness of the original properties of a TEM image (Fig. 15). It should be clear that the readership thereby runs the risk of understanding colour as a fixed property of the virus.

Fig. 14: The New York Times, 'surfaces? Sneezes? Sex? How the Coronavirus Can and Cannot Spread', 2020, source: nytimes.com (Screenshot from October 22, 2022)

the background is blue. This image was published by AMI Images in the year 2015 or before (AMI Images, Science Photo Library [no date]).

18 "The rose and yellow spheres are viral particles, which came from a coronavirus sample collected from one of the first cases in the United States." (ibid.)

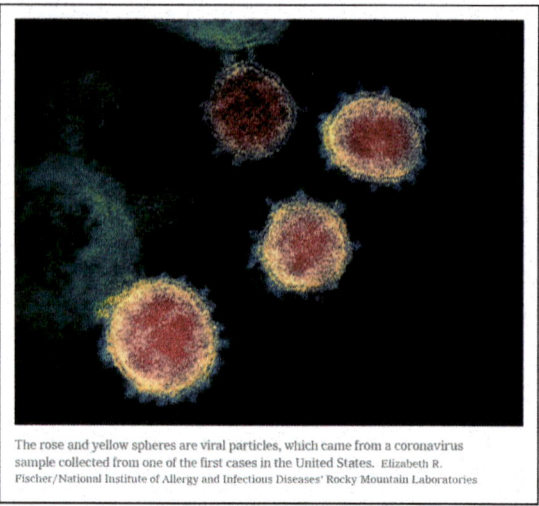

Fig. 15: The New York Times, 'surfaces? Sneezes? Sex? How the Coronavirus Can and Cannot Spread', 2020, source: nytimes.com (Screenshot (Detail) from October 22, 2022)[19]

Finally, in the last two cases mentioned here, computer-generated images were referred to as microscopic images in the captions. This happened in the Viennese newspaper *Wiener Zeitung* (Fig. 16 and Fig. 17) (Stanzl 2020) with the caption "Das Coronavirus Sars-CoV-2 unter dem Mikroskop."[20], as well as in the British newspaper *The Guardian* (Fig. 18 and Fig. 19) (Honigsbaum 2020) with the caption "Covid-19 under a microscope: 'Did scientists and politicians think they were dealing with a type of flu?'". Such incidents can of course have far-reaching consequences, as they have a strong influence on the perceptions of their readers with regard to Covid-19.

---

19 In the caption to this colourised TEM image, the arbitrarily added colours were used as characteristics to describe the virions.
20 Translation: The Sars-CoV-2 coronavirus under the microscope.

Introducing Science through Images   85

Fig. 16: Stanzl, 'Was wir über das Coronavirus wissen', 2020, source: Wiener Zeitung (Screenshot from October 22, 2022)[21]

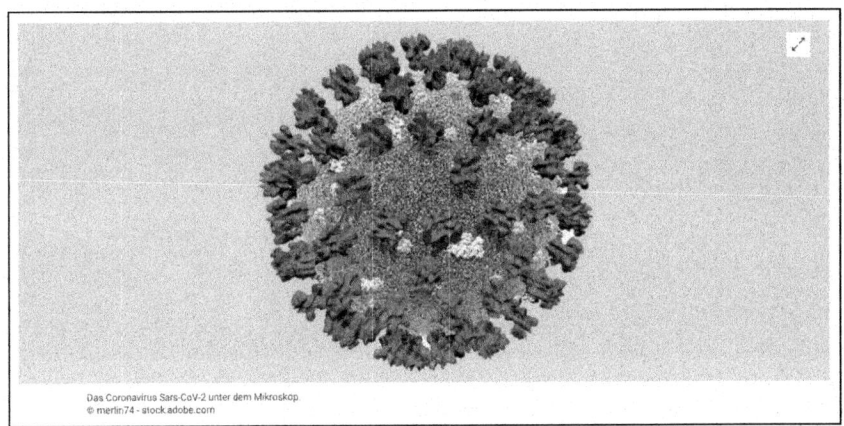

Fig. 17: Stanzl, 'Was wir über das Coronavirus wissen', 2020, source: Wiener Zeitung (Screenshot (Detail) from October 22, 2022)[22]

21 Translation: 'What we know for sure about the coronavirus'.
22 This computer-generated illustration of a virion is referred to as a microscopic image in the caption.

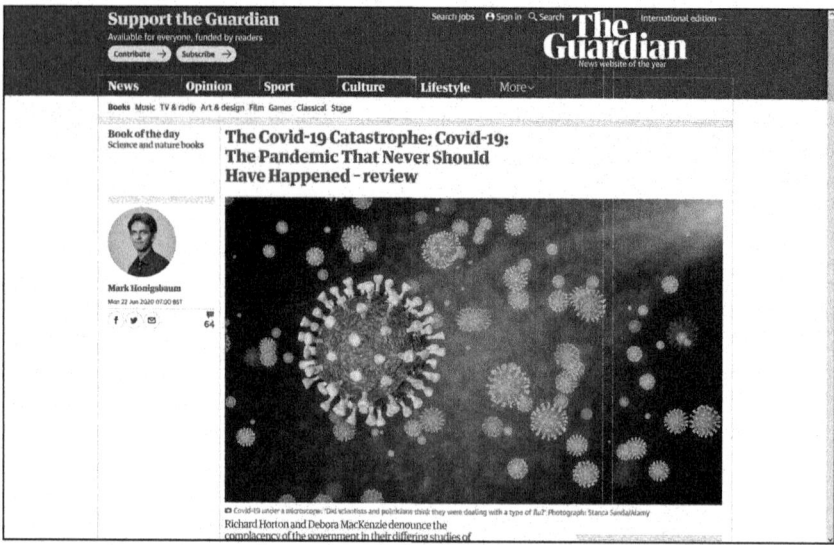

Fig. 18: Honigsbaum, 'The Covid-19 Catastrophe; Covid-19: The Pandemic That Never Should Have Happened – review', 2020, source: The Guardian (Screenshot from October 22, 2022)

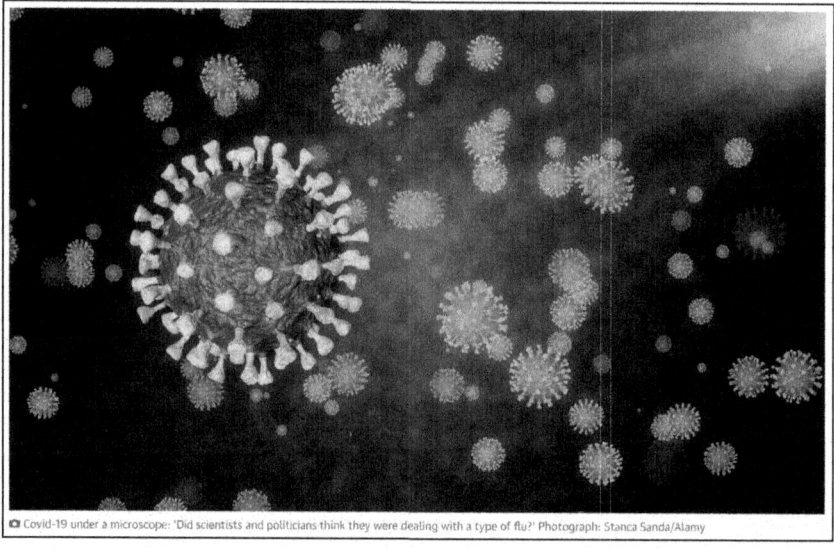

Fig. 19: Honigsbaum, 'The Covid-19 Catastrophe; Covid-19: The Pandemic That Never Should Have Happened – review', 2020, source: The Guardian (Screenshot (Detail) from October 22, 2022)[23]

---

23 Here, too, according to the caption, the image was labelled as Covid-19 under the microscope, although it is an illustration.

Conclusion

From the CDC's handling of Murphy and Whitfield's image, their relation to the definition of archival material, from the history of the creation of the 'spiky blob', and from the recycling and alienation of micrographs by institutions or third parties, the question arises as to what the purpose of popularised microbiological virus representations is and if they still can be 'read' in a scientific context.

If scientific images change their context and are received by a wide audience, they lose their technical codes used in a community of experts. Due to their ambiguous referentiality and their ability to connect to pictorial traditions, the microbiological representations that we have examined in our paper have been suitable not to be read but to be looked at since the popularising dissemination of pandemic viral diseases.

Through our analysis we conclude that popularising effects shape the scientific field itself and that it is impossible to hermetically isolate 'pure' knowledge from the world around it. Apart from the impossibility we consider to be in the separation between 'pure' and popularised knowledge, the intentions and goals behind scientific image production processes play a key role in the development of the final image that will reach the scientific community and the general public in the end.

Based on the selected case studies, we have worked out that the microbiological picture of the virus has been staged for a broader public. The image of the virus relates less to a scientific source and can be seen as a direct consequence of an educational intervention. The popular image of the virus is intended to create drama, it is intended to be frightening, it is intended to have an immediate impact on the viewer, in this sense the educational response is more important than the scientific information.

References

AMI Images Library/Science Photo Library (no date): "Human coronavirus, TEM.". In: "Science Photo Library". Snapshot from: October 4, 2015. Accessed: December 16, 2022. (https://web.archive.org/web/20151004222412/http://www.sciencephoto.com/media/87501/view).

Bradbury, S./ Ford, Brian J./Joy, David C. (2022): "transmission electron microscope". In: *Encyclopedia Britannica*. October 10. Accessed: October 16, 2022. (https://www.britannica.com/technology/transmission-electron-microscope).

Bredekamp, Horst/Vera Dünkel/Birgit Schneider (eds.) (2019): The technical image: a history of styles in scientific imagery. University of Chicago Press.

Brennen, J. Scott/Felix M. Simon/Nielsen, Rasmus Kleis (2021): "Beyond (mis)representation: Visuals in COVID-19 misinformation." In: *The International Journal of Press/Politics* 26.1, 277–299.

Callista Images: "EM Coronavirus, causing SARS - stock photo". In: *Getty Images*. Accessed: October 22, 2022. (https://www.gettyimages.com/detail/photo/coronavirus-causing-sars-royalty-free-image/1134490146).

Callender, Brian/Obuobi, Shirlene/Czerwiec, M. K./Williams, Ian (2020): "COVID-19, comics, and the visual culture of contagion." In: *The Lancet* 396.10257, 1061–1063.

CDC (2005): "SARS-CoV Images". In: *Public Health Image Library* (PHIL). May 3. Snapshot from: January 11, 2012. Accessed: October 21, 2022. (https://web.archive.org/web/20120111023613/https://www.cdc.gov/sars/lab/images.html).

CDC (2017a): "SARS-CoV Images". In: *Public Health Image Library* (PHIL). December 6. Snapshot from: December 9, 2017. Accessed: October 21, 2022. (https://web.archive.org/web/20171209152459/https://www.cdc.gov/sars/lab/images.html).

CDC (2017b): "SARS-CoV Images". In: *Public Health Image Library* (PHIL). December 6. Snapshot from: October 30, 2020. Accessed: October 21, 2022. (https://web.archive.org/web/20201030142026/https://www.cdc.gov/sars/lab/images.html).

CDC (2018): "SARS-CoV Images". In: *Public Health Image Library* (PHIL). Snapshot from: December 8, 2018. Accessed: October 21, 2022. (https://web.archive.org/web/20181208035736/https://www.cdc.gov/sars/lab/images.html).

CDC (2019): "SARS-CoV Images". In: *Public Health Image Library* (PHIL). Snapshot from: April 24, 2019. Accessed: October 21, 2022. (https://web.archive.org/web/20190424085540/https://www.cdc.gov/sars/lab/images.html).

CDC (2020a): "PHIL - Home". In: *Public Health Image Library* (PHIL). Snapshot from: February 5, 2020. Accessed: October 23, 2022. (https://web.archive.org/web/20200205175857/https://phil.cdc.gov/).

CDC (2020b): "SARS-CoV Images". In: *Public Health Image Library* (PHIL). Snapshot from: November 1, 2020. Accessed: October 21, 2022. (https://web.archive.org/web/20201101063436/https://www.cdc.gov/sars/lab/images.html).

CDC (2020c): "SARS-CoV Images". In: *Public Health Image Library* (PHIL). Snapshot from: October 30. Accessed: October 21, 2022. (https://www.cdc.gov/sars/lab/images.html).

CDC (2022): "Home - Public Health Image Library(PHIL).". In: *Public Health Image Library* (PHIL). Accessed: October 19, 2022. (https://phil.cdc.gov/.)

Eckert, Alissa/Higgins, Dan/CDC (2020): "Details, ID#: 23311.". In: *Public Health Image Library* (PHIL). Accessed: October 22, 2022. (https://phil.cdc.gov/Details.aspx?pid=23311).

Hentschel, Klaus (2014): *Visual cultures in science and technology: a comparative history*, USA: Oxford University Press.

Honigsbaum, Mark (2020): "The Covid-19 Catastrophe; Covid-19: The Pandemic That Never Should Have Happened – review.". In: *The Guardian*. June 22. Accessed: October 22, 2022. (https://www.theguardian.com/books/2020/

jun/22/the-covid-19-catastrophe-covid-19-the-pandemic-that-never-should-have-happened-review).

Ludwig-Maximilians-Universität München | Department Biologie | Botanik Ultrastrukturforschung: " Negativkontrastierung Galerie". Accessed: October 16, 2022. (https://www.ultrastruktur.bio.lmu.de/de/forschung/tem/negativkontrast/index.html).

Mallapaty, Smriti (2020): "Should virus-naming rules change during a pandemic?" In: *Nature*. August 6. (https://www.nature.com/articles/d41586-020-02243-2).

Mayer, F./Spiess, E. (1976): "Elektronenmikroskopische Präparationsmethoden Negativkontrastierung." Göttingen.

Mitchell, William John Thomas (2015): *Image science: iconology, visual culture, and media aesthetics*. University of Chicago Press.

Müller, Johannes (1840): *Handbuch der Physiologie des Menschen für Vorlesungen. Zweiter Band*, Coblenz: Verlag von J. Hölscher.

Murphy, Heather (2020): "Surfaces? Sneezes? Sex? How the Coronavirus Can and Cannot Spread". In: *The New York Times*, May 22. Accessed: October 22, 2022. (https://www.nytimes.com/article/coronavirus-how-it-spreads.html).

Murphy, Dr. Fred/Whitfield, Sylvia/CDC (1975a): "Details, ID#: 10270.". In: *Public Health Image Library* (PHIL). October 30, 2017. Snapshot from: Dezember 10, 2017. Accessed: October 16, 2022. (https://web.archive.org/web/20171210161113/https://phil.cdc.gov/Details.aspx?pid=10270).

Murphy, Dr. Fred/Whitfield, Sylvia/CDC (1975b): "Details, ID#: 15523.". In: *Public Health Image Library* (PHIL). October 30, 2017. Snapshot from: Dezember 10, 2017. Accessed: October 16, 2022. (https://web.archive.org/web/20171210161108/https://phil.cdc.gov/Details.aspx?pid=15523).

Murphy, Dr. Fred/Whitfield, Sylvia/CDC (1975c): "Details, ID#: 10270.". In: *Public Health Image Library* (PHIL). Accessed: October 16, 2022. (https://phil.cdc.gov/Details.aspx?pid=10270).

Murphy, Dr. Fred/Whitfield, Sylvia/CDC (1975d): "Details, ID#: 15523.". In: Public Health Image Library (PHIL). Accessed: October 16, 2022. (https://phil.cdc.gov/Details.aspx?pid=15523).

Murphy, Dr. Fred/Whitfield, Sylvia/CDC (2020a): "Details, ID#: 10270.". In: Public Health Image Library (PHIL). Snapshot from: May 14, 2020. Accessed: October 16, 2022. (https://web.archive.org/web/20200514114851/https:/phil.cdc.gov/Details.aspx?pid=10270).

Murphy, Dr. Fred/Whitfield, Sylvia/CDC (2020b): "Details, ID#: 10270.". In: *Public Health Image Library* (PHIL). Snapshot from: October 18, 2020. Accessed: October 16, 2022. (https://web.archive.org/web/20200514114851/https:/phil.cdc.gov/Details.aspx?pid=10270).

Nakagawa, K. /Lokugamage, K.G./Makino, S. (2016): "Chapter Five - Viral and Cellular mRNA Translation in Coronavirus-Infected Cells." In: John Ziebuhr (eds.): *Advances in Virus Research*, Vol. 96: p.165–192. Academic Press. (https://www.sciencedirect.com/science/article/pii/S0065352716300409).

NIAID (2020a): "Novel Coronavirus SARS-CoV-2". In: *Flickr*. February 13. Accessed: October 22, 2022. (https://www.flickr.com/photos/niaid/49530315718).

NIAID (2020b): "Novel Coronavirus SARS-CoV-2". In: *Flickr*. February 14. Accessed: October 22, 2022. (https://www.flickr.com/photos/niaid/49534865371).

Rawsthorn, Alice (2020): "Alissa Eckert on designing the 'spiky blob' Covid-19 medical illustration.". In: Wallpaper*, October: p.174–176. https://www.wallpaper.com/design/design-emergency-alissa-eckert-designs-covid-19-illustration.

Rogers, Kara (2011): "The Eye. The Physiology of Human Perception" In: Britannica Educational Publishing (eds.), *The Human Body*. New York: Britannica Educational Publishing.

Roingeard, P./Raynal, P. I./Eymieux, S./Blanchard, E. (2019): "Virus detection by transmission electron microscopy: Still useful for diagnosis and a plus for biosafety.". In: *Reviews in medical virology* Vol. 29(1). (https://doi.org/10.1002/rmv.2019).

Sjaak de Wit, J. J./Cook, Jane K. A. 2020. "Spotlight on avian coronaviruses." In: Avian Pathology Vol 49 (4): p.313–316. Accessed: October 19, 2022. (https://www.tandfonline.com/doi/full/10.1080/03079457.2020.1761010).

Sliney, D. H. (2016): "What is light? The visible spectrum and beyond.". In: Eye Vol. 30: 222–229. (https://doi.org/10.1038/eye.2015.252).

Stanzl, Eva (2020): "Was wir über das Coronavirus sicher wissen.". In: *Wiener Zeitung*, June 12. Accessed: October 22, 2022. (https://www.wienerzeitung.at/nachrichten/wissen/mensch/2064025-Was-wir-ueber-das-Coronavirus-fix-wissen.html).

Waldman, Gary (2022): *Introduction to light: the physics of light, vision and color*, Mineola, New York: Dover Publications, Inc.

Webster, Michael A. (1996): "Human colour perception and its adaptation" In: *Network: Computation in Neural Systems* 7: p.587–634.

Williams, D.B./Carter, C.B. (2009): *Transmission Electron Microscopy: A Textbook for Materials Science 2*, New York: Springer.

WHO (2020): "Accelerating a safe and effective COVID-19 vaccine.". Accessed: October 22, 2022. (https://www.who.int/emergencies/diseases/novel-coronavirus-2019/global-research-on-novel-coronavirus-2019-ncov/accelerating-a-safe-and-effective-covid-19-vaccine).

Zhu, N./Zhang, D./Wang, W./Li, X./Yang, B./Song, J./Zhao, X./Huang, B./Shi, W./Lu, R./Niu, P./Zhan, F./Ma, X./Wang, D./Xu, W./Wu, G./Gao, G. F./Tan, W./China Novel Coronavirus Investigating and Research Team (2020): "A Novel Coronavirus from Patients with Pneumonia in China, 2019.". In: *The New England journal of medicine*. (https://doi.org/10.1056/NEJMoa2001017).

Activism
and Counter-Narratives

The World Is Falling Apart; But You're Still Coming to Work, Right?
Remote Labour and Memes against Capitalism at the Times of the COVID-19 Pandemic

Christina Tente

Abstract

The article reflects on visualisations and aestheticisations of remote labour, i.e., working from home as a pandemic measure, through Internet photo-based memes. Drawing from Stuart Hall's model of encoding and decoding and using visual discourse analysis, the article reflects critically on humorous approaches to remote labour and performing oneself as a labouring body at the times of COVID-19. It explores the curious social aspects of physical alienation from one's product of labour and colleagues, as well as the entanglement of workplace and private space. There is a paradox at play; there is the potential of convenience and informality, though simultaneously the labouring body is constantly present, potentially surveilled, expected to be always available. In this context, I am fascinated by the ways that this practice is encoded by memes and how these memes can be decoded either as political commentary to the situation or as oppositional / critical. Departing from my ongoing research at the University of Gothenburg, I categorise my empirical material in subclusters based on their theme, aesthetics, and rhetoric. The article thus focuses on remote labour pandemic memes which draw attention to the zoomification of labour: the liquification of space and time, the shared eerie intimacy with the boss and coworkers, the isolation and loneliness or the chaos of sharing the home and workspace, and the performativity of the zoom gaze. Additionally, it discusses remote labour memes which perform a direct critique on neoliberalism, by personifying the capital as the boss figure and by articulating humourous oppositional discourses against the exploitation, perhaps carrying themselves post-capitalist possibilities. In terms of theory, inspiration is drawn by the works of Franco 'Bifo' Berardi and Mark Fisher.

Keywords

memes; labour; remote labour; pandemic; COVID-19; encoding decoding

Introduction

Since the beginning of the COVID-19 pandemic in January 2020, memes satirically responding to the virus have become a regular occurrence on the Internet, generating diverse visual narratives of the new situation. These *unprecedented times* are almost immediately encoded into hashtags, often becoming *viral*, as Internet users create and share memes commenting humorously on various aspects of *being-in-a-pandemic*. From image macros satirising the hoarding of toilet paper to reaction Photoshops drawing attention to quarantine mental health struggles, memes encode and mediate the pandemic into a plethora of images, constituting it an intense, hypervisual, *postphotographic* event. Drawing from Joan Fontcuberta, I approach the pandemic as *postphotographic*, characterised by an overproduction and circulation of visual material, by "hypervisibility and universal voyeurism" (2015: 12), forming an "an era in which images are comprehended through the idea of excess" (ibid). In this postphotographic context, and together with media and social media photography as well as modes of expanded visualities, memes weave visual culture(s) of the COVID-19 pandemic, narrate visual histories of the pandemic, facilitate digital, dislocated communities, while being cultural clusters, sociopolitical discourses, and humorous outlets. By the end of March 2020 most countries in Europe, US, and Canada have transitioned to mainly remote activities mediated by screens and teleconference tools. In spring 2020, memes commenting on *remote labour* emerge. Following various subcategorisations, ranging from Zoom humour and home office outfits to colleague relations on teleconference meetings, *remote labour* memes provide with multimodal commentary on diverse aspects of working from home due to the pandemic. At times, they articulate satirical political commentary and at times, they offer a creative antidote to the fatigue, the uncertainty, and the boredom of living in front of a screen for the better part of the day. Additionally, they (attempt to) make a connection between the global situation, work exploitation, and general precarity of life under capitalism. Other times, they comment on the status of the worker who is considered vulnerable enough to stay at home, but also essential enough to keep working despite the almost apocalyptic situation.

This paper explores encodings and decodings of remote labour as a pandemic measure through photo-based Internet memes produced and disseminated through *Western* social media.[1] I argue that remote labour is a crucial aspect of

---

1   I use the term *Western* with a grain of salt and aware of its problematic generalising content. As *West*, I refer to a diverse and imaginary / constructed geopolitical area consisting of Europe, US, and Canada. All my empirical material comes from anglophone social media, websites, repositories and online communities, and references anglophone popular cultural products. Of course, I do not suggest that there is a *homogenous* West. However, I argue that there is a common and hegemonic neoliberal discourse, which is also articulated explicitly or implicitly through cultural

the pandemic, as it combines living under lockdown (or with social distancing restrictions), work related alienation and precarity, a desire for sociality, and an attempt or (exhausting) obligation to carry on as usual, despite the situation. I propose that memes draw attention to and comment on the collective characteristics of remote labour, and consequently, I suggest that they are themselves political discourses, perhaps even evoking a class consciousness to a *classless*, fragmented, and alienated *precariat* (Standing, 2011).

As part of my ongoing research at the University of Gothenburg, I have collected, annotated, and archived 580 memes from the first year of the pandemic (January – December 2020), using the following sources: websites which post memes (such as BoredPanda, and Buzzfeed), the digital cultural database KnowYourMeme, the meme generator imgflip, private and meme accounts on social media (Reddit, Twitter, Instagram, Facebook) which post content using the tags #coronamemes; #covidmemes; #cancovidmemes; #coronavirusmemes; #2020, and the subreddit /r/CoronavirusMemes/. The materials were further grouped into categories and subclusters according to their theme, rhetoric, and overall (visual) discursive characteristics.[2] One of these categories is *remote labour memes* and consists of 106 images. Consequently, the article refers to memes which aestheticise humorous, satirical, selfreflexive, and relatable commentary on remote labour as one aspect of *being-in-a-pandemic*. I have chosen to present memes which which do not require a certain level of *meme literacy* (Milner, 2012; cf Shifman, 2014a: 100), i.e., not referring to niche audiences but being decodable. Additionally, I have decided to exclude materials which articulate pandemic negationist and conspiracy theorist discourses.[3]

I approach my empirical material departing from Stuart Hall's model of *encoding* and *decoding*, as it was developed in his essays *Encoding and Decoding in the Television Discourse* and *Encoding / Decoding*. Though social media are obviously a much different landscape than the media that Hall analyses, his communication theory offers to this day useful insights in unpacking multimodal discourses. In discussing television as a medium, Hall argues that a message (a comment, a carrier of ideology, a thesis) is encoded into a meaningful discourse

---

products, mainstream and social media. This discourse is also reproduced, satirised, or deconstructed through memes.

2   Other categories: *if 2020 was; toilet paper hoarding; zoom humour; apocalypse outfits; my plans versus 2020; march 2020 versus april 2020; after the quarantine*, et al.

3   Initially, the archive included 621 memes, but I decided to delimit it to 580 by removing conspiracy theorist or other problematic material. By extension, the memes that I have downloaded and included in my sample were not retrieved from pages or private accounts with alt right, far right, or conservative right ideological affiliations. I also removed some material which lacks decodability or, in other words, appeals to niche audiences and requires familiarity with very specific interests to be decoded.

and is mediated to the audiences through institution and societal relations (2001: 509). Hall writes that:

before this message can have an 'effect' (however defined) [...], it must first be appropriated as a meaningful discourse and be meaningfully decoded. It is this set of decoded meanings which 'have an effect', influence, entertain, instruct, or persuade, with very complex perceptual, cognitive, emotional, ideological, or behavioural consequences (ibid).

This model of communication opens space for different ways of decoding a message, i.e., for receiving, appropriating, and accepting or rejecting it. Hall speaks of *dominant / hegemonic* positions, *negotiated*, and *oppositional codes* (2001). In my approach, the message that is encoded into memes is usually already perceived as a *negotiated* or even *oppositional* code to a *dominant* discourse, due to the characteristic of this visual material and the medium that carries it (Internet, social media). Memes may use humour and satire to aestheticise and articulate political discourses and sociocultural commentaries. Satire itself may be a *negotiated* or *oppositional* position to hegemonic discourses, so the meme, carrying a satirical discourse, usually presents itself as not supporting a dominant discourse. I suggest that this also applies to alt right, far right, and conservative meme discourses, for example memes produced by incels, Donald Trump supporters during the time of his presidency, pandemic negationists and antivaxxers in the context of COVID-19. These groups often adopt a self image of being marginalised (even when they are a majority, for example in the case of Trump supporters in 2017), pushed away, deliberately silenced for knowing and propagating a *truth*. In that sense, they present their memetic material as always oppositional to a hegemonic discourse, despite actually being the ones who form the hegemonic discourses.[4] In that sense, memes carry the possibility of articulating radically postcapitalist or progressive as well as extremist conservative or even neofascist discourses, depending on who creates, uses, or abuses them. In the words of Marijn Bril, "memes are self-referential, infinitely reproducible, often semi-anonymous, viral, symbolic, and dank, they become the modern-day icon of intersectional class

---

4   There is currently a lot of scholarship on alt-right, conservative right, and extreme right memes, as well as pandemic (and) conspiracy theories, all of which are often overlapping categories. For a short and insightful analysis on how memers supported Trump's 2017 election, see also Goerzen, Matt (2017), 'Notes toward the memes of production'. In: *Texte Zur Kunst*, Issue No. 16, June 2017, 'The New New Left', available at https://www.textezurkunst.de/en/106/notes-toward-memes-production/#id15 (accessed 2 February 2022). A really good and recent article on conspiracy memes is Hernandez Aguilar, L. M. (2023). Memeing a conspiracy theory: On the biopolitical compression of the great replacement conspiracy theories. *Ethnography*, 0(0). https://doi.org/10.1177/14661381221146983 (accessed 2 February 2022).

criticism while at times exploring polarizing conversations through extreme-right rhetoric" (2022: 181). Having teased the topic, it is now time to define the empirical material as well as the term remote labour and dive into the analysis.

Remote Labour Memes. Definitions and Delimitations

The term *meme* was introduced and defined by biologist Richard Dawkins in 1976, as "small cultural units of transmission, analogous to genes, that spread from person to person by copying or imitation" (Shifman, 2014a: 9). The term itself derives from Greek (*mimema* / μίμημα, i.e., imitated), and is a word play with *gene*. For Dawkins, much like genes, memes are replicators which "undergo variation, competition, selection, and retention" (ibid). Memes predate the digital era, yet they are revived both as cultural medium and as a term with the advent of the Web 2.0, to a large extend due to their participatory character (Shifman, 2014a: 18). Limor Shifman suggests that memes may be approached as cluster units rather than singularities and defines them as:

(a) a group of digital items sharing common characteristics of content, form, and/or stance, which (b) were created with awareness of each other, and (c) were circulated, imitated, and/ or transformed via the Internet by many users (2014a: 41).

There are various meme genres including photo and text assemblages, as well as videoclips. In this article, I refer to photo-based Internet memes, i.e., memes which recontextualise photographs for their iconic parts. Photo-based memes push the borders of photography and toy with the medium's (contested) indexicality. As Limor Shifman writes, such memes deconstruct photography's *truthfulness* in a multifaceted manner while being modes of *hypersignification* (2014b: 344) [5]. Through their visibly manipulated aesthetics, they focus on "revealing the constructedness of mediated images" (2014b: 347). Shifman calls their "predigital incarnations" *iconic photos* (ibid). In that sense, photo-based memes may as well be approached as *hypericonic photos*.

Additionally, memes are based on imitation and replication (Shifman, 2014a: 19), and their authorship or origin story is often unclear. With humour, irony, and subversive appropriations of visual material, they encode sociopolitical and cultural commentary into decodable pictures, sometimes referring to products of

---

5   An exaggerated example of *hypersignification* is the case of *shitposting* with its deliberately bad resolution and purposefully sloppy editing. Mike Watson (2022) refers to *shitposting* as "inspiring a descent into a trash visual culture whereby jokey, low resolution, and glitched productions are seen as inherently more valuable than the serious and polished output of the mainstream media" (30).

pop visual culture and other times creating their own emerging visual cultures.[6] Their decodability is a result of their attempt to address the reader / viewer directly, by illustrating a certain situation as relatable and almost universal. Furthermore, they may be ephemeral and respond to current political, social, and cultural contexts through diverse angles. Pandemic memes are such an example. As the virus would evolve and the pandemic would progress, the digital visual encodings of this experience would also mutate. For instance, one of the earliest recurring meme themes that I have detected already traces back to the end of January and beginning of February 2020, commenting on the high levels of contagiousness of the virus and how it would spread so rapidly through excessive travelling. A recurring joke in memes of this pandemic phase is that people would normally stay indoors to heal from a common cold but keep travelling while being sick with the new virus. And this is only the beginning. Throughout 2020, memes respond to various aspects of the pandemic, encoding life in lockdown, quarantine fashion (or apocalypse outfits), life after lockdown, the advent of the second wave and the list goes on. Memes are part of the digital participatory culture (Shifman, 2014a: 172), commodities weaving visual cultures which have their own economies of circulation (*sharing*) and assessment (*like, upvote*). As an integral part of the digital ecosystem, they function as what Nathan Jurgenson calls *social photo*. Departing from Jurgenson, I approach memes as photographic images created for and disseminated by the social media ecosystems as means for "communicating an experience" (2019: 32), turning the "ephemeral into something tangible, and our life into something collectable, consumable" (46), and emerging as "part of a preexisting and expanding will to document" (52). In line with this, they play a crucial role in the visual narrative(s) of the COVID-19 pandemic.

Finally, a photo-based meme consists of an iconic and a linguistic part, i.e., one or more images and a text which includes a caption. I approach the relationship between these two parts as symbiotic and complementary. The linguistic part contextualises the iconic, while the iconic part aestheticises, supports, and implements the punchline, while making it relatable to the reader. The picture that is used for the iconic part is accessible and decodable, which makes the meme easy to read, share, and replicate. In discussing semiotics and signs, Hall refers to the iconic as "particularly vulnerable to being 'read' as natural because visual codes of perception are very widely distributed and because this type of sign is less arbitrary than the linguistic" (2001: 512). Departing from that, I argue that

---

[6] Most of the memes that are discussed in this article are all recontextualisations of products of pop culture, i.e., stills from films, series, pop characters. A good example of the emergence of a pop culture (or quasi pop culture) through memes is characters like Doomer and Doomgirl, which also emerged during the pandemic. On the Doomer macro, see also, Watson, Mike (2022). *The Memeing of Mark Fisher*, Zero books, pp. 88–90.

the iconic part in a meme is rather read as *hyperreal* both on a symbolic / theoretical and on an aesthetic level; an abstraction, a "real without origin or reality" (Baudrillard, 2011: 5), which reterritorialises and manipulates existing pictures using subversive, exaggerated, often maximalist aesthetics.

The above are central in my approach to the empirical material, i.e., pandemic remote labour memes. As *remote labour*, I refer to the practice of working from home in the context of the global pandemic and with the use of teleconference software and hardware, i.e., screens, cameras, microphones, platforms such as Zoom, Microsoft Teams, Google Meet etc. I distinguish between pandemic remote labour and working from home in general, as I approach the former as a (seemingly) temporary COVID-19 measure and the latter as a long term and prepandemic practice. Before COVID-19, working from home usually refers to office jobs and may be presented as a practice that the worker has chosen for themselves. In Melissa Gregg's thorough research (2012), working from home is a practice often marketed as allowing the worker to adjust their work schedule. It *sells* flexibility and a sense of freedom of movement; one can take breaks to stretch or leave the house for a while (Gregg, 2012: 3).

While some [*workers*] see wider social benefits, including environmental considerations, their reflections are typically more personal, and include regular indictments of office culture that conspire to create an unhealthy work environment. Ambient lighting, freedom of movement, and lack of stress are among the major benefits cited when working out of office (2012: 40).

It also *sells* productivity; no coworkers may mean less distractions and better time management, and in the end, this is what corporate capitalism desires.[7] The positive attributes are often highlighted to conceal the exploitation and the colonising of the private space and time.[8] Working from home is packaged as a practice beneficial to the worker, and as an opportunity to be thankful for.

On a first level, it might seem as though working from home and pandemic remote labour are the same thing. Obviously, they share similarities; besides, they both refer to working from home. They are both tied to and defined by the technologies that enable them. They are both convenient as well as exploitative; one may theoretically organise their home office and working schedule as they see fit, however the liquification of space and time constitute them always quasi-available. Additionally, they both impose an extra burden to the worker, which is the responsibility to have the technological means to perform their work from home. Needless

---

7   Also, obviously no coworkers means less or even no opportunities to unionise.
8   Melissa Gregg's research, which departs from accounts of people working from home, discusses this liquification of boundaries between work life and home life. She also refers to the difficulty of defining what constitutes working and what does not, using as an example the answering of work emails while at home (5–7).

to say, they impose the financial weight of utilities and electricity. Another shared characteristic is the aspect of surveillance. Neither of these two work practices are panoptic, however there may be a sense of constant surveillance especially in cases of teleconferencing. At the same time, this sense can be circumvented by turning off the camera and microphone function, by withdrawing from the action while remaining 'logged in', 'visible', present though absent.

However, remote labour in the context of the pandemic is quite different, mostly due to its non voluntary character, and as it does not entail merits such as a freedom of movement or lack of stress. A global pandemic without a visible endpoint is not exactly a stress-free condition and the lockdowns, the curfews, and the social distancing mandates complicate or limit mobility. Additionally, in spring 2020 remote labour is either imposed or offered as a possibility, but either way it is not really something that is chosen for convenience. It is either imposed or chosen as a preventative measure, as an attempt to stay safe and *flatten the curve*. The motivation is responsibility and anxiety, the very real fear of getting sick or becoming the *patient zero* in a workspace. Additionally, in contrast to previous home office practices, remote labour also refers to jobs that would otherwise have been performed away from home, like teaching, coaching a workout session, or performing a music concert. It is also characterised by a sense of ephemerality and vagueness. Furthermore, remote labour is usually accompanied by narratives of individual responsibility and (perhaps inadvertent) classism. As many countries adopted a categorisation of *essential* and *non essential* workers, remote labour as a measure underlines job hierarchies and imbalances. It is a practice aimed to protect, but it cannot be practiced by everyone, so the hypervulnerable *essential* workers are still exposed. Remote labour is an example of capitalist realism, as Mark Fisher (2009) defines it, indicating that, while everything seems to be falling apart, the neoliberal cogs shall keep turning. The pandemic is an extreme situation, often pictured as an apocalyptic event, an event that could force the system to collapse. But it is easier to imagine the end of the world than the end of capitalism, so remote labour offers a way of resuming business until that *end of times* arrives, and perhaps even beyond.[9] The memes that comment on this aspect of the pandemic toy a lot with this apocalyptic aspect of the pandemic and the dystopic elements of remote labour.

The empirical materials that I have gathered indicate the decoding of various aspects of remote labour and from different angles. Some meme subclusters focus on the exploitation and satirise the boss archetype, while others comment ironically on the alleged laziness of working from home. Other meme subclusters draw attention to the isolation and others criticise the technological aspects of remote

---

9   This phrase appears as the title of the first chapter in Mark Fisher's book *Capitalist Realism*. According to Fisher, the phrase is attributed both to Fredric Jameson and to Slavoj Žižek (2).

labour, by joking about glitches or failures to mute oneself. As the material is quite diverse, in the following pages, I will only refer to the subclusters which focus on general characteristics of remote labour: memes that discuss the liquification of space and time and the isolation, and memes that criticise the exploitative absurdity of the situation.

What Day Is It? Zoomification, Isolation, Collapsing of Space and Time

In 2009, Franco 'Bifo' Berardi wrote on emerging technologies changing labour practices, which feels quite relevant in describing the 2020 digital workspace. In *The soul at work*, Berardi argues that, with the advent of the mobile phone, the worker is no longer in control of their time, and constantly expected to be available. The phone may ring at any time and the worker is supposed to answer (2009a: 89–90). Berardi calls this *celluralisation*. The worker is tied to the mobile phone, while the workday is fragmented into cells of worktime, undefinable, unregulated, never ending. I argue that remote labour is beyond *celluralisation*. If mobile phone technologies transformed the labour landscape in the 1990s, then teleconferencing technologies are transforming the pandemic labour landscape. This is not necessarily ad hoc negative, as there may be interesting possibilities in the use of teleconferencing tools, provided that they are regulated and used critically. However, with the global pandemic as pretense and with an overuse of teleconferencing tools, remote labour fashions a dystopic work environment, an upgraded version of Berardi's celluralisation. The labourer is not only expected to be always available, the lockdown and measures also make it unavoidable, as home is work and work is home.

Inspired by Berardi, and using Zoom as a metonymy, I argue that remote labour is defined by *zoomification*. The term is a figure of speech, based on the colloquial use of Zoom as a noun and a verb to refer to various types of cyber-encounters. The use of this software became so widespread during the pandemic, that the word itself came to signify digital meetings and encounters, even when the software itself was not used.[10] An example of this trend is that the exhaustion caused by online hyper-activity has been named *Zoom fatigue*. Geert Lovink describes the causes of this condition as "the brain's attempt to compensate for the lack of full body, non-verbal communication cues; a sense of constant self-

---

10   This is nothing new; a few years back, Skype was often used as a verb and a noun to metonymically refer to digital encounters. In this article, the use of Zoom as a metonymy is by no means a critique on the software, but a comment on the general overuse of teleconferencing technologies in the context of the pandemic, which leads to exhaustion and exploitation.

consciousness; engagement in multiple activities with no real focus; and a consistent tugging temptation to multi-task". (Lovink, 2020: n.p.). In *zoomification* the distinction between work and private space and time dissolves; the labourer is a priori available at any time, as they have nowhere else to be. There are no excuses; there is a deadly virus roaming the streets and a mandate to stay indoors, there is no commuting time to delay them, the workers do not even need to get dressed and ready for the workday. The technology makes it easier, almost eliminating preparation time and offering the ability to work from the comfort of one's living room. A dystopic (pseudo)sense of convenience, which conceals the fact that this is still a workspace, with hierarchies and struggles. Additionally, this is not regulated and there is no collective physicality which would work as a support network. There is no room to linger, no physical collectivity, no physical common area to socialise with the colleagues.

The collapsing of space and time, the merging of workday and privacy, the fatigue that characterise remote labour and *zoomification* are recurring themes in the memes. An obvious joke aestheticised in memes is the inability to distinguish between days, due to repetitiveness and identicality.

Fig. 1: *Meme found in April 2020 as retweeted from private account on Twitter (original poster missing). Information about the meme template: https://knowyourmeme.com/memes/what-year-is-it (accessed February 22, 2023).*

In Fig. 1, the iconic element is that of a man with long messy hair and beard, visibly dirty and distressed. This is a recognisable image of actor Robin Williams portraying the leading character in the film *Jumanji* (1995). An alternative version of this meme uses a screenshot from *Cast Away* (2000), depicting a raggedy Tom Hanks with dirty long hair and beard. In both cases, the original picture and its connotations influences the ways that the meme can be decoded. Familiarity with the films constitutes the message more easily decodable, and the use of these characters as encodings of the remote labourer further contextualises the precarious state of the latter. By using the image of dirty, lonely, distressed isolated characters who have lost sense of time, these memes comment on the confusion and physical sloppiness that accompanies remote labour isolation. In Fig. 1, the inability to distinguish between days is further encoded in the caption, which is a reterritorialisation of an original quote from the film. Williams' character is released from the board game and immediately asks what year it is, being unable to tell exactly how long he was kept in the world of Jumanji. The quote here is changed into "what day is it?" and the caption is "a month into working from home". As every day is identical and as work is performed without detours and entanglements with other bodies, time melts away. Remote labour together with isolation, makes the workday relative and undefinable. The workers do not have agency over their own time because, as Berardi argues, time "is separated from the social existence of the people who make it available to the recombinative cyber-productive circuit" (2009b: 33).

Apart from time, in remote labour, presence is liminal too. The labouring bodies, sharing a hyperreal digital workspace, are simultaneously present and absent, often oblivious to each other's physicality. At the same time, as remote labour is performed from home, this imaginary cyberencounter is diffused into the labourers' physical private spaces, making the encounter intimate and eerie. There is a hyperreal entanglement of presence and absence, or rather a *failure of presence* and *failure of absence* as Mark Fisher describes it (2016: 83). In its relation to teleconference technologies, remote labour is *hauntological*, collapsing space and time (Fisher, 2012: 8). The teleconference *room* has no walls and no windows, it is immaterial and hyperreal; yet it opens a door of one's physical room and (forcefully) lets the colleagues and bosses in. There is a sense of always being watched, often by people one has never met in *real* life or with whom the relationship should have remained strictly professional. The gaze feels penetrative, and intimacy feels forced, unsolicited; one's boss is *inside* one's living room, glimpsing fragments of the everyday life. There is a possibility to blur the background, use filters, or turn off the camera. Nevertheless, this does not eliminate the hauntological eeriness of a spectral presence; the gaze of the humans present in the call may have been blocked, but what about the nonhuman gaze, i.e., bugs, algorithms, and all the other invisible watchers. Søren Pold calls this the *Zoomopticon*: "the condition in which you cannot see if somebody or something is watching you, but it might be the case that you're being watched by both people and corporate software" (cf Lovink, 2020: n.p.). Byung-Chul Han calls this *digital feudalism and surveillance* (p. 89). There are ways to circumvent or to minimise this surveillance, but it is impossible to become completely ellusive.

Yet with the camera on, labour may become (even) more performative. One becomes more aware of their gestures and facial expressions, one may feel the need to *seem* involved and present. The interesting part is that one does not really know if they are being watched, but may still adopt an excessive performativity. I have come across memes which encode this performativity in two antithetical ways; memes which playfully comment on the act of *looking at oneself* (Fig. 2), and memes which draw attention to the performativity by eliminating it, by encoding what happens when the camera is off (Fig. 3). The first case decodes the gaze which (re)turns towards oneself. The worker may keep checking themselves on the screen to see of they are being perfomative enough. This may have adverse effects, as they may become entrapped by their own image and disengage from the zoom event itself; is this *zoom narcissism?* Fig. 2, a meme based off of actor Jason Sudeikis looking at himself during the digital 2021 Golden Globes, is an example of this type of memes. The iconic part is simple aesthetically and discursively, the caption is clear; it could address anyone who is currently practicing remote labour. Additionally, it indicates awareness; the remote labourer knows that they are looking at their own reflection during the meeting, but they cannnot stop, they get immersed in it. This meme exists in many variation, including both stills from films or series and known meme templates or stock character macros, such as the *awkward look monkey puppet*.[11] Based on this type of material, I suggest that zoom performativity seems to be quite a common practice and "zoom narcissism" does not happen unconsciously, but rather, out of an impulse or a conscious need or even a desire to *show* and to *perform* engagement.

Fig. 2: Meme originally found on subreddit selfies of the soul, /r/me_irl, in March 2021. The comments also indicate awareness and seem to authenticate the meme's decodability and accessibility. Source: https://www.reddit.com/r/me_irl/comments/lzdqzl/me_irl/ (accessed February 22, 2023).

---

11   For more information on this template, see https://knowyourmeme.com/memes/awkward-look-monkey-puppet (accessed February 22 2023).

me on zoom with the camera disabled

Fig. 3: Recontextualised screenshot from Seinfeld, using the character George Costanza as an encoding of the remote worker and as a memetic example of flawed masculinity (Shifman, 2014a). Meme originally found on a private account on Facebook as a repost (original poster missing).

On Zoom meeting
Boss : We can't hear you i think your mic might be off
Me:

Fig. 4: Meme using a photo of rapper 50 cent sleeping as a joke to remote labour's alleged escapability, found in April 2020 on a private account on Facebook as a repost (original poster missing).

As for the memes which satirise what happens when the camera is off, this subcluster either decodes the sloppiness and raggedy-ness of remote labour (Fig.3) or comically imply that a turned-off camera is also a chance to slack off (Fig. 4). These may be approached as oppositional memetic discourses to remote labour and as hint that *zoomification* and *zoomopticon* may be circumvented by turning off the camera and microphone. Here, the "solution" is embedded in the "problem". Either way, when the camera is off, there is no need for excessive performativity and a relaxed, informal, slow atmosphere may be assumed. This informality may translate to a lack of dresscode (Fig. 3) or even a reclaiming of one's time and space (Fig. 4). At the same time, this subcluster of remote labour memes often perform a tongue-in-cheek comment on how remote labour conditions paired with the precarity of being-in-a-pandemic affect mental health. For example, Fig. 5 depicts four different characters captioned as "work from home video calls be like". Three of them are comically half-dressed and one appears as dirty and startled in front of her laptop screen. The workers in these memes appear both as not caring for their physical appearance (i.e., assuming a relaxed, informal atmosphere) and as not having the mental energy to get dressed for work as they normally would. The iconic in these memes oscillates between comfort and withdrawal, indicating bodies on the verge of mental collapse. The punchline can be read simultaneously as a joke on the liberty of remote labour dress code, and as a dark humorous comment on fatigue and depression.

Fig. 5: Multi-image meme panel which uses screenshots from four television series (named in the picture), originally found on private account on Instagram in April 2020 (original poster missing). Probably created by a corporate account, due to its format and font.

This meme exists in many variations. I have come across a four-panel image meme portraying actor Matthew McConaughey, progressively looking less formal and more comfortable as the days of remote labour go by. This version juxtaposes four photos of the actor; the first two, marked as Day 1 and Day 2, portray him dressed in a tuxedo and smiling confidently. The last two, marked as Day 3 and Day 4, are images of characters that he has played, and portray him as sloppy and on the verge of a breakdown. Another version of the meme juxtaposes two pictures of actor Chris Hemsworth. The first picture, entitled "working from home day 1" portrays Hemsworth well-groomed and clean, whereas the second picture, entitled "working from home day 2", portrays him with long messy hair and a beard, raggedy and sloppy. Both cases satirise the melting of time and remote labour exhaustion by using the image of two famous male actors, considered conventionally attractive for heteronormative Western-centric standards.[12] In both cases, lack of effort or energy and progressive deterioration of physical and mental state as the pandemic and remote labour continue, is underlined through the iconic. By focusing on their progressive deterioration, the memes aim for relatability and humorously imply that this situation affects everyone involved. It echoes a phrase from 'Bifo' Berardi's *Precarious Rhapsody*, where he argues that "precariousness is no longer a marginal and provisional characteristic, but it is the general form of the labor relation in a productive, digitalized sphere, reticular and recombinative" (2009b: 31).

So far, the memes of this category imply that the labourer is living alone. In the examples that I chose to share as well as in the majority of empirical material in my sample, there are no visible indications of symbiosis (human or transspecies), and the only encounters seem to be performed digitally, visually, in a disembodied fashion. I argue that this may be a sociopolitical comment on isolation, work related exhaustion, and mental health struggles, already serious issues which worsened due to the pandemic. Though this joke may seem like a sidenote, it is a crucial political comment, addressing the relation between isolation, mental health, and capitalist work environments, with the added layer of the pandemic isolation and precarity. The struggle is not individual and random, but collective and influenced by the general precarious state. Mark Fisher writes on *Capitalist Realism* that the system "The 'mental health plague' in capitalist societies would suggest that, instead of being the only social system that works, capitalism is inherently dysfunctional and that the cost of it appearing to work is very high" (2009: 19). Here, the memes encode a serious and multifaceted issue in a sarcastic and relatable way, by visualising the exhaustion in one's appearance and by omitting presence of symbionts. They do this by illustrating lonely and lonesome characters who do not have the strength and motivation to get dressed and washed up, and who cannot even tell the difference between days as every day is experienced as identical due to isolation, work exploitation, and lack of contact.[13] The memes

---

12   The aspect of gender is also interesting. These two examples refer to conventionally attractive men "deterriorating" (in patriarchal, heteronormative, and sexist standards). As Limor Shifman suggests, memes often toy with the idea of a *flawed masculinity* (2014a: 76) – and this seems to be the case here. *Flawed masculinity* is also encodable in Fig.3, which departs from an image of George Costanza (*Seinfeld*, 1989–1998), who was the personification of televised flawed masculinity in the 1990s.

13   It is worth to mention that mental health and depression memes are a rather large genre. A good analysis of this genre is provided by Scherz, Lauren (2022). 'I'm not lonely, I have Memes. The cognitive (dis)embodied experience of depression memes'. In: Chloë Arkenbout, Laurence Scherz (eds), *Critical Meme Reader II. Memetic Tacti-*

address the reader and viewer directly, as though they refer to each viewer alone, creating a sense of inclusivity (*the message is addressed to everyone*) as well as exclusivity (*the message is addressed to you*).

Nevertheless, it is crucial to note that not all remote labour memes depart from living alone, nor do they all comment on potential depression. Quite a different effect is created by remote labour memes which picture the worker isolating together with children or pets. Here the emphasis is no longer placed on the mental health struggles of isolation and the liquification of space and time. Children remote labour memes encode the chaos of simultaneously working and caring for a child while having limited mobility. Instead of spectrality, liquification, and haziness, they mediate a hectic atmosphere, a chaotic physicality, a comical "despair". I suggest that these memes have a light and sympathetic tone, rather than the bleak melancholy and dark humour of the previous set of memes. Their primary focus is not on remote labour, but on parenthood at the times of a global pandemic. On a similar note, pet memes are quite soothing and often encode the remote labour condition from the animal symbiont's point of view. They may indicate how happy the symbiont is when the human stays at home, or, alternatively, they may illustrate the presence of a pet during a zoom call and how uplifting this may be for the coworkers. I argue that these memes toy with the concept of emotional support animals, being themselves *emotional support memes*. Finally, some of these remote labour pet memes depart from original photographs of pets *styled* in such a way to appear that they are also working from home. I suggest this type of memes are a COVID-19 related and upgraded version of the LOL Cats meme genre, i.e., pictures of cats (various pets in that case) "accompanied by systematically misspelled captions which typically refer to the situation shown in the photo" (Shifman, 2014a: 110). They may be approached as apolitical or lacking depth, though their cultural role is more significant than that, encoding "a level of choice and a level of freedom of expression that just doesn't merit being ignored or belittled" (Watson, 2019: 103).

In this section, I analysed examples of COVID-19 memes which comment on aspects of pandemic remote labour by drawing attention to the (further) liquification of space and time, the mental health struggles that stem from isolation, and I briefly mentioned memes commenting on the chaotic aspects of the symbiosis with young children and pets. These examples encode sociopolitical commentary to an exploitative situation, but they do not address the issue directly. In the last part of this article, I refer to memes which adopt an oppositional approach to the exploitation, and I briefly reflect on what possibilities such an approach may open.

cality, Institute of Network Cultures, Amsterdam, pp. 352–375. Mike Watson also discusses this genre thoroughly and insightfully in *The Memeing of Mark Fisher* (2022).

... but You're Still Coming to Work, Right?

With the advent of the pandemic and the subsequent turn to *zoomification*, an older meme theme re-emerges. I am referring to memes which consist of an image of doom and catastrophe, accompanied by the caption "...but you're still coming to work, right?". The joke is aesthetically and discursively self explanatory and the decoding is obvious. This meme theme is known as *bosses be like* and illustrates unreasonable employer demands, by pairing the caption with a disaster photograph, for example a car buried in snow or sunken in flood water. The meme predates the pandemic, and this indicates that remote labour as well as general working conditions follow a pattern of deterioration. I suggest that the recurrent emergence of these memes during the pandemic is a political commentary on the working conditions in late capitalism and an oppositional discourse to capitalist realism. The pandemic is not the focus, but the apocalyptic background which should have changed everything. Nevertheless, the exploitation continues (or even deteriorates). In these cases, the memes encode the worsening remote and *essential* labour conditions during the pandemic.

Fig. 6: An example of "...but you're still coming to work right?" type of meme, recreated and reposted by various accounts in various time periods. This version is from March 2020.

In this type of memes, capitalist realism and exploitation are not immaterial or intangible concepts, but fleshy entities, human (or anthropomorphous) agents. The invisible hand of the market is the visible hand of the boss figure. A characteristic example is Fig. 6, which departs from a screenshot from *Star Wars Episode V* (1980). The image and the punchline indicate a world falling apart, accompanied by the capital's request to resume business as usual. The figure of the boss or the personification of the capital is here portrayed as an evil Sith Lord. The meme portrays a society burning and the Sith boss figure walking across the ashes to approach the relic of the worker and ask if they are still coming to work. This meme's origin is uncertain, but it was first created before the pandemic. While searching for metadata, I noticed that the exact same meme appears to have been created and uploaded on imgflip by different accounts seven, four, and two years ago.[14] The fact that the exact same meme seems to be created by different accounts is telling of the medium's replicability, or in the words of Limor Shifman, "reproduction via copying and imitation" (2014a: 18). Memes start from an original idea and disseminate vastly, often being elevated into a broader discourse, a social phenomenon. Shifman writes:

First, memes may best be understood as pieces of *cultural information that pass along from person to person, but gradually scale into a shared social phenomenon.* [...] A second attribute of memes is that they reproduce by *various means of repackaging* or *imitation*. (2014a: 18–19, original emphasis).

This is an example of how difficult it often is to track down the original poster and to attribute authorship to a meme creator. Additionally, it indicates awareness and an ongoing dialogue between and across various memers, which identify the same issue and use the same or similar modalities to problematise it. I argue that the "…but you're still coming to work" memes before the pandemic emerge with natural catastrophes, such as hurricanes, and are used to comment on capitalist realism, the lack of empathy, and the capital's *misanthropic drive* (Han, 2021: 122). Consequently, they (re)emerge during the pandemic for the same reason, yet this time they have a larger audience to refer to, as the state of precariousness is even more generalised. Apart from remote labour, these memes also comment on the separation between essential and non essential workers and satirically encode the practice of still physically showing up to work despite the severity of the situation.

Aesthetically, in discussing the precarity of essential workers, these memes often reterritorialise material from postapocalyptic science fiction. For example, Fig. 7 recontextualises a still from the film *I Am Legend* (2007), indicating a collapsed society, and the figure of one (and perhaps the only) human survivor with his dog, walking through the destroyed streets of a deserted metropolis.[15] The caption is "me when my boss still calls me into work during the Coronavirus outbreak. / You're still coming to work, right?". The meme encodes the physical

---

14   The oldest entries registered on imgflip are from seven years ago. The version that I included in my sample was found on Reddit via Google search (*pandemic work memes*) in March 2020.

15   Interestingly, during the second year of the pandemic and with the advent of vaccines, the film was heavily memeified by pandemic negationists and antivaxxers, as it departs from a vaccine which turned everyone into zombies.

precariousness of essential workers, while making an ironic joke with the title of the film (I am *legend*) and the hegemonic discourses articulated during the pandemic by the state, the capital, and the media on the essential workers' *heroism*. It may be decoded as a disguised commentary to the essential workers being thanked for their service, while being overworked, underpaid, and overexposed to the SARS-CoV-2 virus with insufficient safety measures. The memes in this category may comment sarcastically on capitalist realism. Mark Fisher argues that, after having occupied the horizon of the thinkable, capitalism has also colonised the dream life (2009: 8–9), and these memes echo this colonisation. The pandemic is being portrayed as an apocalyptic event; and despite this apocalyptic background, the essential worker is still expected to physically show up at work. There may seem like nothing is left, yet the capital cogs are still turning, as there are still those who profit.

Fig. 7: Meme based off a screenshot from the film I Am Legend (2007). Found as a repost from a private account on Instagram. Original poster missing.

I suggest that the memes in Fig. 6 and Fig. 7, while referring both to essential and remote workers, both imply an employer who is so immersed in class privilege, that they are ignorant and naïve. Unaware of or oblivious to the level of the catastrophe, they take the workers' labour as a given. This is a relatively mild critique. Other memes of this broader category are more direct in their criticism by encoding the boss figure as a sadistic supervillain, receiving pleasure in exploitation. The figure of Thanos from the Marvel Cinematic Universe is prominent in that case, being one of the most powerful and destructive supervillains in the pop cultural references of the time.[16] Additionally, memes using the image macro 'and then I said' (also known as 'rich men laughing', Fig. 8) also form a good example of directly oppositional memetic discourses. In this case, the boss figure is a group of white bourgeoise men, who are laughing, wearing suits, and holding drinks and cigars. Two of the men in the picture are recognised as Ronald Reagan and George Bush; this is the epitome of encoding a neoliberal boss figure.[17] The meme exists in many variations and the caption always starts with the phrase "and then I said" or "and then I wrote". In Fig. 8, the caption "and then I wrote 'we care about your health and wellbeing during these unprecedented times'" refers both to insincere empathy on behalf of the capital and on neoliberalism's attempts to monetise the pandemic and not lose profit by adopting a rhetoric of *caring* while exploiting the workers. Here the critique is focused on the ways the 'we are all in this together' narrative which is adopted by those higher in the hierarchies in order to create an illusion of equality and unity to mask the power structures. The meme here encodes class privilege and draws attention to this false and forced rhetoric of equality. As Rosi Braidotti writes, "not all humans are equal and the human is not a neutral category. It is rather a normative category that indexes access to privileges and entitlements" (2020: 466). Braidotti's posthuman approach draws attention to the inequalities and privileges, including the issue of class and work hierarchies that is encoded in this meme theme. This meme is thus a political commentary on capitalist realism.

The memes of this category carry a bittersweet atmosphere, as the captions echo a harsh reality which stretches beyond the pandemic. Additionally, I argue that this subcluster indicates awareness and consciousness on behalf of the workers. The question is whether this awareness results in acceptance and resignation, or in assuming subversive possibilities. This is a question that I cannot answer, at least not in the scope of this article. However, I propose that the creation and dissemination of remote labour memes is in *itself* a discussion on remote labour, working conditions at the time of the pandemic, and capitalist exploitation in general – and this is the realisation of a subversive possibility. The meme itself

---

16 Thanos is also both used as a visual metonymy of the SARS-CoV-2 virus in pandemic memes and as a visual metonymy to that which will defeat the virus (for example, vaccines in the memes generated between November 2020 and January 2021).

17 The origin of this meme template dates back to 2011. According to KnowYourMemes, "on July 25th, 2011, Redditor raks1991 submitted a post titled "We told them.." to the /r/pics subreddit, featuring a photo of several politicians, including Ronald Reagan and George Bush Sr., and the caption "We told them wealth/ would 'trickle down'!" [...] The original photo was taken by Time magazine photographer Diana Walker after Walter Cronkite interviewed President Ronald Reagan at the Oval Office on March 3rd, 1981" (source: https://knowyourmeme.com/memes/and-then-i-said). Thus the first registered meme that was created with this template was indeed a meme commenting on neoliberalism.

is a political discourse, a digital assembly point for those participating in remote labour, and perhaps a facilitator of class consciousness for a fragmented precarious class. 'Bifo' Berardi's comments on the *virtual class* are relevant here: this is a class of "those who do not identify with any class, since they are not socially or materially structured: their definition depends on the removal of their own social corporeality" (2009b: 104). Furthermore, Berardi introduces the *cognitariat*, which is 'the social corporeality of cognitive labor' (2009b: 105), "the semiotic labor flow, socially spread and fragmented" (ibid). I argue that remote workers are a virtual class which may become cognitariat, provided that the collective identity is realised and conjured. As this experience has been magnified in the context of the pandemic and as it is encoded into memes, its reception and decoding may generate intimacy and togetherness, a methexis, a realisation that the struggle is not individual, that there is collectivity despite the fragmentation and the dislocatedness.

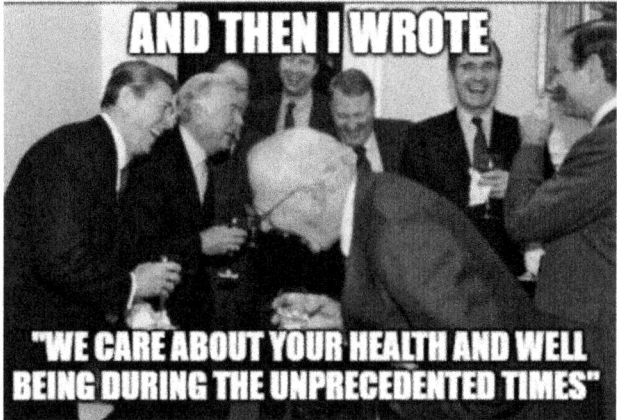

Fig. 8: 'And then I wrote' meme, sent privately to me via Instagram. Original poster missing. More information on the meme template: https://knowyourmeme.com/memes/and-then-i-said.

To conclude, I suggest that if used critically and properly, the memes may have the possibility to draw attention to the collectivity and evoke class consciousness. These possibilities depart from the characteristics of the medium, i.e., the accessibility, decodability, and reproducibility. Slavoj Žižek approaches the memes as viruses, both dead and alive, driven by the urge to reproduce and to populate (2020: 79–80). According to Žižek, this is a characteristic shared between SARS-CoV-2, memes, and capital; the latter being a "virtual entity which doesn't exist in reality independently of us. It exists only insofar as we, humans, participate in the capitalist process" (p. 110). Žižek is aware of the power as well as the limitations that these three spectral entities have. They can mutate, spread and *infect*, they can bring changes, but they can also be contained, diverted, hibernated, perhaps eradicated. There are potentials but there are also limitations, as memes, *despite* their subversive and counter hegemonic aspects, are still part of the digital ecosystem, as well as part of the broader politicoeconomic system, themselves being commodities and data. Nevertheless, a critical approach to creating, using, disseminating memes facilitates participatory and, perhaps, antihierarchical digital visual cultures, which in turn enable awareness and engagement. Mike Watson calls for a *slow meme movement* "that encourages use of the internet's great resources in a considered way that challenges the data economy while building a community that can also function and *meet offline*" (2022: 39, *emphasis added*). Watson's approach assumes a *postcapitalist* position, defined by Mark Fisher as a victory that will come *through* capitalism (2020: 55, *original emphasis*). Fisher's conceptualisation of postcapitalism develops *"from* capitalism and moves *beyond* capitalism. Therefore, we're not required to imagine a *sheer alterity*, a *pure* outside. [...]. We can begin with, work with, the pleasures of capitalism, as well as its oppressions" (Fisher, 2020: 55–56). In that sense, the oppressive structures themselves may theoretically provide with the means of pleasure and empowerment (i.e., the memes) and function as a point of departure for encounters, preferably in *offline* modes.

Conclusion

In this article, I outlined some key characteristics of remote labour and discussed aspects such as *zoomification*, isolation, and exploitation through photo-based Internet memes. With visual discourse analysis and departing from Stuart Hall's model of encoding and decoding, I grouped my empirical material in subclusters based on their theme, aesthetics, and rhetoric. These subclusters were further analysed in order to form an understanding of how memes may satirise and criticise problematic aspects of remote labour. As the empirical material suggests, remote labour pandemic memes draw attention to the liquification of space and time, the shared eerie intimacy with the boss and coworkers, the isolation and loneliness or the chaos of sharing the home and workspace, and the performativity of the zoom gaze. Additionally, remote labour memes often perform a direct or indirect critique on capitalism, by personifying the capital as the boss figure and by articulating humourous oppositional discourses towards the exploitation. The latter type of memes is openly oppositional and quite bleak, illustrating a generalised and progressively deteriorating condition. Departing from this latter subcluster, I reflected on postcapitalist possibilities through critical uses, though emphasising the importance of *offline encounters*.

Films and series referenced in the memes

Seinfeld (1989–1998, tv series): cr. Jerry Seinfeld, Larry David, net. NBC, TBS.
I Am Lagend (2007, film): dir. Frances Lawrence, prod. Village Roadshow Pictures et al., distr. Warner Bros Pictures.
Jumanji (1995, film): dir. Joe Johnston, prod. TriStar Pictures et al., distr. Sony Pictures Releasing.
Star Wars V: The Empire Strikes Back (1980, film): dir. Irvin Kershner, prod. Lucasfilm Ltd., distr. 20th Century Fox.

References

Baudrillard, Jean (1995): *Simulacra and Simulation*. Transl. Sheila Glaser. The University of Michigan Press.
Braidotti, Rosi (2020): "'We'Are In This Together, But We Are Not One and the Same". In: *Journal of Bioethical Inquiry* 17, pp. 465–46.
Berardi, Franco 'Bifo' (2009a): *The Soul at Work. From alienation to autonomy*. Los Angeles: Semiotext(e). Translated by Francesca Cadel & Giuseppina Mecchia.
Berardi, Franco 'Bifo' (2009b): *Precarious Rhapsody*. London: Minor Compositions. Translated by Arianna Bove et al.
Bril, Marjin (2022): "Memes in the Gallery: A party inside an image ecology" In: Arkenbout, C. & Scherz, L. (ed.), *Critical Meme Reader II. Memetic Tacticality*. Amsterdam: Institute of Network Cultures.
Goerzen, Matt (2017), "Notes toward the memes of production." In: *Texte Zur Kunst*, Issue No. 16, June 2017, 'The New New Left', available at https://www.textezurkunst.de/en/106/notes-toward-memes-production/#id15 (accessed 2 February 2022).
Fisher, Mark (2009): *Capitalist Realism. Is there no alternative?* UK: zero books
Fisher, Mark (2012): "What is Hauntology?". In: *Film Quarterly*, 66/1, pp. 16–24.
Fisher, Mark (2016): *The Weird and the Eerie*. London: Repeater.
Fisher, Mark (2020): *Postcapitalist Desire: The Final Lectures*. London: Repeater. Ed. Matt Colquhoun.
Fontcuberta, Joan (2015): *The Postphotographic Condition*. Montreal: Le mois de la photo à Montréal.
Gregg, Melissa (2012): *Work's intimacy*. Polity.
Hall, Stuart (2001): "Encoding, Decoding." In: Simon During (ed.), *The Cultural Studies Reader*. London: Routledge.
Han, Buyung-Chul (2021): *Capitalism and the death drive*. Polity.
Jurgenson, Nathan (2019): *The social photo*. London, New York: Verso.
"Know your meme"[website]. https://knowyourmeme.com/. Accessed February 21, 2023.

Lovink, Geert (2020): "The anatomy of Zoom fatigue." In: *Eurozine*. Published 2 November 2020. https://www.eurozine.com/the-anatomy-of-zoom-fatigue/#anchor-footnote-21. Accessed February 22 2023.

Shifman, Limor (2014a): *Memes in Digital Culture*. Cambridge, Massachusetts: The MIT Press.

Shifman, Limor (2014b): "The cultural logic of photo-based meme genres." In: *Journal of Visual Culture*. Vol. 13(3), pp. 340–358. DOI 10.1177/1470412914546577.

Standing, Guy (2011). *The Precariat*. London: Bloomsbury Academic.

Watson, Mike (2019): *Can the Left learn to meme?* Zero books.

Watson, Mike (2022): *The memeing of Mark Fisher*. Zero books.

Žižek, Slavoj (2020): *Pandemic!* New York: Polity.

Installation Art in Virtual Reality

Charlotte Kent

Abstract

Despite its inconsistent appeal, VR won't disappear, especially with transnational technology corporations embracing it as the social space of the future, emphasized by the social distancing required of the recent COVID pandemic and anxieties of ones to come. Examining individually the works of Carla Gannis and Kurt Hentschlagger that were developed during the first year of the COVID lockdown, I explain how these works invoke many of the psychological and phenomenological conditions identified by Claire Bishop in Installation Art (2012) as pertinent to that art practice. I propose the term digital installation to assist audiences in perceiving these new digital spaces through the affective and intellectual lens of the more familiar, though still disconcerting, context of installation art rather than the currently popular approach of naming them via the corporate name of the social VR platform, such as Mozilla Hubs. By bringing these works produced on social VR platforms into a discussion of installation, I emphasize how these works invoke a set of physical and psychological experiences for participants that have kinship with the decentering effect of installation. I conclude with a performance by Matthew Gantt in a space designed by Claudia Hart to lead into the exploration conducive to resisting corporate interests and economies that are rapidly adopting VR for their dreams of a 'metaverse.' Hybrid experience is our reality and artists' use of VR offers a space in which to examine what that sociality might be, distinct from the designed interactions provided by the private labeling of corporate spaces.

Keywords

Covid-19 pandemic, contemporary art, installation art, media art, virtual reality, metaverse.

Discussing the use of Virtual Reality (VR) in art—especially how to label it, how to define it, how to discuss its materiality—challenges even the most adept new media scholars. Despite its inconsistent appeal, VR won't disappear, especially with transnational technology corporations embracing it as the social space of the future, commonly referred to as a "metaverse." The social distancing required of the recent COVID pandemic alongside anxieties of ones to come propel research and development. With blockchain enabling digital transactions of currency and digital objects and AI increasing productivity, VR provides the environment for these social engagements—a trifecta whose utilities and values are united under the umbrella term Web3. An emphasis around virtual experiences undermines the far more relevant hybridity of our experience. The social norms and prejudices of the tangible world appear in virtual spaces and the experiences of virtuality shift how we understand or behave in tangible contexts. Artists' use of VR offers a space in which to examine what this new hybrid sociality might be, distinct from the designed interactions provided by the private labeling of corporate spaces. I propose the term digital installation to assist audiences in perceiving these spaces through the affective and intellectual lens of the more familiar, though still disconcerting, context of installation art. With reference to Claire Bishop's text *Installation Art* (2012), I present how the works of Carla Gannis, Kurt Hentschlagger that were produced during the first year of the COVID lockdown, raise similar issues as classic examples of installation art, in order to then conclude with an example by Claudia Hart and Matthew Gantt relevant to the performative nature of social interactions.

Bishop's text *Installation Art* (2012) provides much of the grounding for this essay and she opens her text explaining that "installation art is a term that loosely refers to the type of art into which the viewer physically enters, and which is often described as 'theatrical', 'immersive', or 'experiential'" (Bishop 2016: 6). Those are precisely the same terms that are frequently used around artists' works in virtual reality which likewise "addresses the viewer directly as a literal presence in the space," a feature she identifies as a key characteristic of installation art (ibid.). The embodied presence of the viewer shifts away from the objective distance proffered typically by painting or sculpture (with recognition that any number of writers have expounded on the immersivity that occurs in sitting with a work of art for a length of time) (Clark 2006; Findlay 2012). The experience of social VR requires participation and I not only visited the spaces discussed in this article, but in some instances performed or spoke to audiences in them. After first drawing relations between VR and installation art, I will use many of Bishop's argument around installation art to examine individually the works of Carla Gannis, Kurt Hentschlagger, and the collaborative work of Claudia Hart and Matthew Gantt that were developed during the first year of the COVID lockdown. I conclude by addressing the importance of this as corporate interests and economies adopt VR for their dreams of a 'metaverse.'

Virtual Reality as Digital Installation

For those who are not ready to commit to the complex world of video games, digital artists' projects are proving to be one of the most accessible means of exploring virtual reality (VR). VR can be solitary or social, as in multi-player online video games. Though social VR has been around for a while, amidst the period of social distancing and remote access, it became an ideal space for connecting to share a joint experience. The quarantine requirements of COVID-19 brought increased attention to the use of social VR, which includes game environments, business meeting rooms, counseling support spaces, and creative installations by artists. The term indicates a virtual environment in which people are meant to interact with each other. The artist designs the space, but audiences have some autonomy in their movements within the context of the work, so that it operates in many ways like an installation.

In 1999, the media scholar Ken Hillis described VR as "a hybrid term. It refers to an individual experience constituted within technology, and it draws together the world of technology and its ability to represent nature with the broad and overlapping spheres of social relations and meaning" (Hillis 1999: xv). Though the *Oxford Encyclopedia of Aesthetics* claims that VR "necessarily explores degrees of realism and of verisimilitude," even if those realms are fantastical, the emphasis on realism minimizes other values (Kelly 2008: 444). Some artists explore abstraction (Kent 2022). Some projects seek to cultivate psychological conditions, such as the United Nations' initiative around VR in 2015 that aimed "to bring the world's most pressing challenges home to decision makers and global citizens around the world, pushing the bounds of empathy," according to the website (United Nations). Their application of realism in this instance also has socio-political consequences.

Known for its headsets, VR appears in different formats. HMDs (Head Mounted Displays) require "computers, head mounted displays, body-tracker sensors, specialized interfaces, and 3D graphics" (Rizzo Koenig 2017: 878). Stereoscopic projection screens, as in a CAVE (Computer Automated Virtual Environment) provide another form of immersive VR. But non-immersive virtual reality also exists in the more basic gaming situation: someone seated in front of a screen with 3D graphics and a user interface through a pad, joystick or mouse. VR is a medium with these three variants and its goal according to one writer is to "perceptually replace the outside world with the virtual world to psychologically engage users with simulated digital content" (Rizzo Koenig 2017: 878).

Despite their offerings of virtual experiences, most VR projects were tethered to a local computer drive until online systems developed the power to run these high-demand interactive graphics simultaneously for multiple participants, enabling greater sociality. Given the broad understanding and wide array of applications, the term social VR seems both too general and too specific for many art projects. On one hand, social VR includes the social interactions necessary for such game spaces as Roblox or World of Warcraft, as well as those spaces created by artists for particular occasions. On the other hand, referencing VR narrows it to be understood merely in terms of its technology, whereas its style, narrative, or timescape may be equally meaningful frames of reference for artists. Because VR remains new to many audiences, its association can be enticing or off-putting, but either way it typically arouses a superficial curiosity. These projects can be taken less seriously by general audiences because people associate VR with a technology in progress (Hillis 1999: xxi).

Mozilla Hubs is a popular social VR space in part because the screen experience works well for those who don't have access to headgear; the virtual collaboration platform works in a browser and people can create their own 3D spaces or join ones that already exist. These can be simply decorated 'rooms' or complex layered creations. Many of the artists in this article specified Mozilla Hubs in presenting their work, which offers some understanding of the technical infrastructure underlying the work, but likewise reinforces the commercial entity. Unless there is a compelling reason to identify Gamblin paint or Photoshop, why should the technical means be emphasized? The argument that the different platform have specific keystrokes and gestures used to navigate these spaces applies but instructions can be provided at the entry point without having to label the entire artwork with the corporate brand.[1] Especially given the corporatization of online social spaces that is occurring as an extension of the capital pouring into constructing the 'metaverse,' corporate labeling seems problematic. My goal is to shift away from a kind of techno-fetishism that insists on examining virtual reality works in terms of their technical proficiencies and consider their social considerations— not least of which have to do with the social distance instantiated by a global pandemic when these projects became particularly popular. The term digital installation can help audiences engage these spaces through the affective and intellectual lens of the more familiar, though still disconcerting, context of installation art.

Rosalind Krauss warns against easy historicizing in her classic essay "Sculpture in the Expanded Field" (1979: 33):

"The new is made comfortable by being made familiar, since it is seen as having gradually evolved from the forms of the past. Historicism works on the new and different to diminish newness and mitigate difference. It makes a place for change in our experience by evoking the model of evolution."

It would be false to claim that social VR has some defined lineage out of installation art. Other influences pervade (Grau 2003; Lanier 2017; Smith 2007). I am not claiming that all VR—or even all social VR—is a virtual instantiation of installation art; some VR operates as film or game. Rather, I am arguing that some projects using social VR platforms aim to produce experiences akin to those that installation art cultivates. Claire Bishop positions installation art in terms of four key areas, which equally illluminate virtual environments: psychology, phenom-

---

1   Mozilla Hubs provides a webpage with keyboard shortcuts to assorted motions, interactions, and other experiences. https://hubs.mozilla.com/docs/hubs-controls.html Any artist may add additional elements in the way they code their particular space, but this list provides a solid grounding.

enology, social politics, TK. Those helpfully expand the field of references and influences, facilities and felicities associated with VR.

Rarely does VR afford sensory immediacy—although haptic gloves and suits seek to provide that—but participation and an awareness of self and others is duly present, just as it is in installation art. Embodiment is a crucial topic in the development of VR and artists speak to the task of grounding their audience. Works ranging from Char Davies' *Osmose* (1995) to Maria Kozak's *Be Still* (2020) play with the values of sensation and bodily control of the participant. There are distinctions to be drawn between virtual and tangible experiences, but VR can also raise audience's awareness of self-presence and context, as cultivated in classic instances of installation art.

Amidst the profusion of viewing rooms that galleries developed when the SARS-COVID-19 virus required businesses to close around the world in March 2020, many artists with technology practices developed virtual galleries through which audiences could observe their work. These spaces became framing devices for digitally rendered works. They were opportunities for gatherings in relation to the art, and opportunities to rethink web-based sociality. These social VR spaces were more interactive than 360-degree viewing rooms, but I am not invoking them as installations *per se*. Bishop is likewise clear in distinguishing how installation art coincides with the rise of installation images and the blurring of the work of art from its presentation (Bishop 2012: 6).

Bishop addresses the difficulty of engaging installation art that has not been experienced and the same is true of digital installations: image stills and filmed sections do not sufficiently convey the experience (Bishop 2012: 10–11). The same is frequently cited about any art and yet installation art is an extreme example of this. This article therefore focuses on specific experiences I had in three digital installations and will examine them each in turn. I attended the opening of Carla Gannis' *Wwwunderkammer* when she transformed the computer based VR space into one accessible from any computer for her solo exhibition with Telematic Gallery; she continued to expand that world, producing chambers in response to the research of various digital culture scholars and professionals. I entered Kurt Hentschlagger's *No Exit Oasis* (2020) through a VR headset with no one else in his studio or the dark immersive world at that time. I attended a performance by Matthew Gantt *Welcome to the Doll's House* (2020) in Claudia Hart's *A Doll's House* (2020), and then participated in an event Hart organized in her *Machiavelli Room* (2021). In Gannis' work, I was in a shared space, speaking to others about the work we were observing. In Hentschlagger's, I was alone, contemplating my experience as such. For the Gantt performance, I was an audience member, whose movement was encouraged from the start of the piece, which is why Hart emphasizes the performativity of being in these spaces.

The sociality is a crucial component, even when alone because these are public spaces. The invitation to the Gantt performance was in a public online forum so there were passersby who had unexpectedly joined and were trying to understand what they were experiencing. These are spaces, in other words, that are partly about reflecting on how we socialize online. Their immersion is a significant feature and requires participation; they undermine efforts at being merely observational spaces in no small part because entering the space often requires donning an avatar, most of which are cartoony but invoke some kind of physical presence—at the very least, ghostly hands to indicate hand controls. Sound is spatially oriented, so greater distance from the sound effect makes it quieter. These elements, however, do not require density and avatars can move through each other, walls, and anything else that does not have a designed limit on it. We are both embodied and disembodied beings in these spaces but that very disembodiment seems to raise considerations of bodily respect and netiquette.

By bringing these works produced on social VR platforms into a discussion of installation, I wish to emphasize several things. First, these works invoke a set of physical and psychological experiences for participants that have kinship with the decentring effect of installation. Secondly, articulating these virtual reality experiences as digital installations may help audiences contextualize the disorienting or merely unusual sensations of being in these spaces. Thirdly, the discourse around art and technology doesn't need to remain alienated from the traditional art historical narrative but has an opportunity in finding relations to ask the traditional narrative to reconsider its arcs in order to better incorporate technology across its global and millennial arcs. Much of this paper focuses on the first point to identify relations between these examples of social VR and installation art, but in so doing aims to introduce how a term like digital installation may frame the experience for those art audiences who are not committed to digital art. I will address the last point in my conclusion.

Curious Spaces: Exploring with Carla Gannis

Telematic Gallery presented a new body of work by Carla Gannis on March 14, 2020 and then promptly closed. A global pandemic of a little understood virus produced rolling closures for businesses and institutions across the United States starting in March 2020. The gallery displayed boxes of curios and sculptural works as well as a "holodeck" in which people could enter her virtual reality "curiosity cabinet" that she had populated with contemporary versions of traditional collections. *Wwwunderkammer* was a response to Gannis' growing XR practice in which she reimagined traditional curiosity cabinets in the context of VR and internet spaces. What was at first a single room would generate three for the gallery's online experience, and then continue to multiply.

Gannis' original VR piece for the exhibition was titled *Wwwunderkammer* and ran on desktop VR with massive CPU & GPU, in full 3D with all of the avatars animated. She had to redesign it to become web-based, so that audiences could access it from anywhere. In that sense, the project truly became public, a shift away from the institutional and private context of the gallery. Much installation art has had this political concern, with ties to institutional critique (Bishop 2012: 102–106). Gannis simulated the Telematic Gallery exhibit space and created a runway into the ever growing *Wwwunderkammer* so that the digital installation provided three rooms to explore: the "Wwwunderkammer Main Room," with assorted cabinets along the perimeter of the room filled with objects to examine; the "Game Cabinet Castle," which worked as a runway into the Main Room but now offers access to many other *Wwwunderkammer* spaces she has subsequently built; and a simulation of the Telematic gallery so that audiences could experience the curated exhibition as it would have appeared in that space.[2] These spaces played on the design of curiosity cabinets, special spaces filled with objects to examine (Fig. 1).

Fig. 1: Carla Gannis, "wwwunderkammer: main chamber," metaverse installation, dimensions variable, 2020, Courtesy of the Artist

The 16th century furor for cabinets of curiosities sought insight into the world, and set precedents in many ways for museum collections, but is also an apt approach to the internet of the 21st century. Every wall and cubby of the "Wwwunderkammer Main Room" is full of the curious artefacts of our era, contemporary versions of traditional collections. Gannis filled The Cabinet of Emerging Technology and

---

2   I italicize the overall, ever-expanding project known as the Wwwunderkammer and put in quotations the chamber with the cabinets that she titled "Wwwunderkammer Main Room." This room operated as a conceptual anchor but "The Game Cabinet Castle" became a de facto main room since it provides audiences selection and access to different chambers that Gannis has since created.

The Cabinet of Obsolete Technology, in the "Wwwunderkammer Main Room" with familiar objects; they prompt us to consider how easy it is to situate a technology in one place or another. Obsolete technologies get rediscovered after all. Instagram copied the design of the Polaroid, but may well be responsible for the recent enthusiasm and re-release of Polaroid cameras and film. Virtual Reality has its own rollercoaster story over the last fifty years described eloquently by Jaron Lanier in *Dawn of the New Everything: Encounters with Reality and Virtual Reality* (2017). Oliver Grau in *Virtual Art: From Illusion to Immersion* (2004) and Matthew Wilson Smith in *The Total Work of Art: From Bayreuth to Cyberspace* (2007) positions VR within a historical lineage of creative developments and tempers the hyped newness of it. The way Gannis produces these curiosity cabinets into virtual reality makes real the question: are we majestic spectators of the wwwunderkammer, or (more likely) part and parcel of it (Fig. 2)?

Fig. 2: Carla Gannis,"Theory of Everything," mixed media cabinet of curiosity, 71" x 32" x 12", 2020, Courtesy of the Artist

Looking at these cabinets may be a solitary experience, and yet they cultivate questions and conversation. This included memories with similar objects in the tangible world, exploration of what one thinks about these objects, but also a free-associative attraction to the array of objects. I found myself browsing the bookshelf, identifying which I had read. As Bishop writes, "we imaginatively project ourselves onto an immersive scene that requires creative free association in order to articulate its meaning; in order to do this, the installations are assemblaged elements are taken one by one and read 'symbolically'" (Bishop 2012: 106). With Gannis' *Wwwunderkammer*, audiences gravitate to some cabinets and objects, particular rooms and experiences, developing their own narratives around the project.

Curiosity cabinets were designated spaces for looking. They decontextualized objects as a part of an intellectual endeavor to observe, analyze, discern and categorize. Collectors sought to have a representative selection of flora and fauna, as well as mechanical curios for their curiosity cabinets (Koeppe 2002). The animal world was a popular feature of curiosity cabinets with collectors including skeletons and drawings, so Gannis introduces a large whale gently undulating beneath the ceiling. It nods to the first illustration of a cabinet of curiosity, Ferrante Imperato's *Dell'Historia Naturale* (Naples 1599) that shows a ceiling covered in fishes. It also invokes the New York City Natural History Museum's famously display in its Hall of Fishes. In so doing, Gannis visualizes the ties articulated in the literature about how curiosity cabinets were forerunners of museums to bring them into the virtual space. It also, however, asserts some of her environmental concerns. In her Instagram post on July 23, 2020 as she was redesigning the project, she quotes the agriculturist Cary Fowler: "To many people, 'biodiversity' is almost synonymous with the word 'nature,' and 'nature' brings to mind steamy forests and the big creatures that dwell there. Fair enough. But biodiversity is so much more than that, for it encompasses not only diversity of species, but also the diversity within species." In the "Wwwunderkammer Main Room," she has dedicated spaces for The Cabinet of Endangered and Emerging Species to help audiences consider what we are losing alongside what we are designing and developing across the sciences. The looking generates interest and concern about the world beyond the cabinet.

Where the cataloging impulse of curiosity cabinets was understood as neutral and guided by scientific observation for many centuries, recent scholarship has put that in question (Graham et al 2005: 31). Gannis' *Wwwunderkammer*, in all its permutations, asks audiences to reflect on certain frameworks and ideologies that get produced through display scenarios. Bishop describes installation art as fulfilling the goal of institutional critique's attempt to expand perspectives: "installation art, by using an entire space that must be circumnavigated to be seen, came to provide a direct analogy for the desirability of multiple perspectives on a single situation" (Bishop 2012: 35). This came to be associated with an "emancipatory liberal politics" because of the multiple perspectives produced through mobility in most installation art (Bishop 2012: 54). Activating the viewer in the space became a part of the politics wherein audiences are responsible for their actions, behaviors, choices in a public space, thus emphasizing their overall social responsibility. The installation and performance artist Mary Kelley's writings identify "a connection between single point perspective and (patriarchal) ideology, and implies that installation art is one way to challenge and subvert this association" (Bishop 2012: 36). Intersectional feminism is a strong undercurrent in Gannis work which she activates by introducing many voices and perspectives in her work. Seven symbolic post-human agents (avatars) inhabit the *Wwwunderkammer*, through which she conducts interviews with humans (represented as avatars in VR) who share their research, stories, art or personal experiences related to specific themes. In this way, Gannis even fractures her own position in the space (Fig. 3).

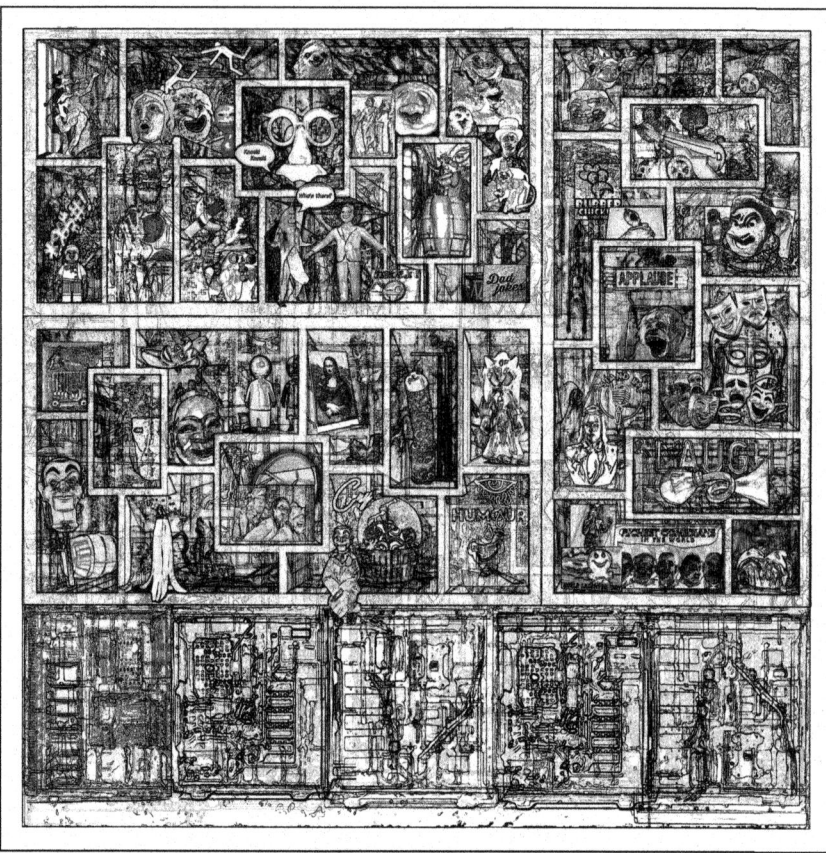

Fig. 3: Carla Gannis, "Study for the Cabinet of Humor as Salve," mixed media drawing, 14" x 13.8," 2020, Courtesy of the Artist

Gannis builds new cabinets in collaboration with others ideas, truly decentering her own perspective. Kabakov proposed that installations should be "a kaleidoscope of innumerable paintings" and the visualizations of VR rendered on a screen exemplify that; there is no framework to limit what the eye beholds (Bishop 2012: 16). *Wwwunderkammer* now includes spaces developed out of the ideas and collaborative effort of artists, specialists, activists and scholars like Regina Harsanyi, Regine Gilbert, Leah Roh, among others; I contributed my research into the absurd for one space. She invites insights from scholars and creatives in the digital landscape. Regina Harsanyi is a much respected media art specialist and conservator whose work with international galleries, institutions and independent artists ensure that media works will be adequately preserved given the easy degeneration of much digital material. An interview produced by one of Gannis' avatars in conversation with Harsanyi about her work in preservation is accessible in the chamber (or on Vimeo) (Gannis) (Fig. 4).

Fig. 4: Carla Gannis, "Is this Chamber Still Supported: Regina Harsanyi," metaverse installation, dimensions variable, 2021, Courtesy of the Artist.

Spotlighting figures in this way is the kind of strong feminist gesture that harkens back to such projects as Judy Chicago's *Dinner Party* (1974–9) with its recognition of the many female artists whose work contributed to that feminist moment. Gannis references the installations of Jessica Stockholder, Judith Barry, and the boxes of Barbara Bloom as influencing how she construed the potential of creating spaces and positioning engagements for audiences.[3] Recognizing these female legacies and influences is important to shifting the patriarchal designations that typically litter citations and references, as evident even in my own history of VR above. The artist and critic Mira Schor made this argument years ago and yet artists of any gender struggle to find diverse influences because of the limited representation of women in the discourse, including Bishop's own text (Schor 1991– 2: 98–118).

The *Wwwunderkammer* spaces aren't designed as interactive in the sense that the audience completes the work but rather as spaces of reflection filled with material for the attendee to use as points of departure. The politics shift from interactivity as a model of political engagement, which is suspect, to one of engagement between the individual and the work. Though this may seem to produce a

---

3   Email with artist, September 2, 2021.

one-to-one engagement, the social context of the spaces and the inability to fixate the work in terms of only one object means both subject and reference object are recognized to be parts of larger communities, both individually and communally situated. Though this is disorienting, it establishes a liminality that is relevant to our current condition.

As Bishop describes the notion of the pragmatist philosopher John Dewey argument in *Art as Experience* (1934): "we can only develop as human beings if we actively inquire into and interact with our environment. Being thrust into new circumstances means having to re-organize our repertoire of responses accordingly and this in turn enlarges our capacity for experience" (Bishop 2012: 24). These spaces are opportunities to examine what an immersive online sociology might be. How will we exist, imagine ourselves, present ourselves in the spaces so much a part of the meta-verse. Spaces like *Wwwunderkammer* offer a chance to explore what we might want social spaces to offer before embracing the claims and designs of transnational tech companies.

The Politics of Phenomenology with Kurt Hentschlager

The artist Kurt Hentschlager has a history of producing "extreme perceptual effects, composed from light, sound and fog. These works physiologically affect the viewer's experience," as he describes on his website (Hentschlagger 2021). His works are typically installed in spaces as large as a warehouse or planetariums that can handle the detailed material production requirements for the experiences he produces. *No Exit Oasis* (2020) is his first work in VR produced in response to the quarantining required of COVID-19 and the cancellation of various shows. He cultivated a way for people to share space where the phenomenological encounter is personal rather than a means of interacting with other humans or machines. *No Exit Oasis* is a space in which to be alone, even though other people can appear in the space and may be visible. He does not know how often that may have occurred as there was no intention to track that when he produced the piece.[4] As with many earlier works, there is no start or end point, and audiences can enter and leave at will (Fig. 5).

VR undoubtedly mediates, and yet Hetschalgger's work doesn't pretend to reproduce a recognizable tangible world. The objects in *No Exit Oasis* are large and unwieldy, evocative of dream structures. There is a large rock formation that operates like an island; it was originally a warped and deformed cardboard box that Hentschlagger 3D scanned, intrigued by its form. A smaller island rock is another 3D scan from a piece of driftwood he found along Lake Superior. There are low-poly, pixelated heads based on 3D scans of African sculptures and objects

---

4   Conversation with artist, October 20th, 2021.

he discovered while staying at the Roger Brown House in Michigan, a residence associated with The School of the Art Institute of Chicago. While excavating the land around his house to plant a garden in the spring COVID quarantine, he discovered a cast iron candle holder; the land was a former dump site and strange objects were frequently unearthed. This was one of the few he kept. He describes the pleasure in playing with scale in a virtual environment: "in a 3D environment scale is relative, thus small objects originally can be made enormous and vice the versa. As well as things without former relation can be mixed and montaged."[5]

Fig. 1. & 2: Kurt Hentschlager, NO EXIT OASIS, 2021, web-based virtual reality on Mozilla Hubs

5   Email to Author February 2, 2022.

Objects in the dark space come from his archive of references, but half-submerged in water and made much larger, they eradicate any semblance to their original formation. Such peculiarities suggest a dream but with a heightened awareness of one's senses produced by the overall darkness with faint sound emanating from the barely lit objects. This is an effect frequently cultivated by many light installation artists, like Turrell. Here, the undulating water had the well-known effect of slowing my breath (Fernandez et al 2019: 1). I was aware of my own dimensionality perhaps because there was so little else in the space to focus upon. Motions became more considered and talking disruptive, even after exiting the VR space. As these responses unfolded, the consciousness of being in a digital stratum made more stark the difference between this space and so many other online environments, even ones as common as landing on a webpage. No flashing lights or bright colors. No demands or ads. Interactivity, though technically present given my motility, otherwise seemed beside the point.

Such intense self-awareness may have been too much for some individuals experiencing the quarantining of the COVID period in isolation, but amidst the incessant group zoom meetings and expansion of online engagements and tools, the quietude raised awareness of a general lack of anything like this online. How could there be? The corporatization of online space and demands for social engagement typically produce design requirements that cultivate perpetual albeit temporary attention (Crary 2014). It is no doubt partly my own interest in digital culture that created this line of thought as the work's sensory phenomena are democratically available to anyone in the space. No intellection is necessary to experience the dark, hushed environment. But, any time floating through the space elicits questions: where am I? What am I looking at? What is going on? These would seem to imply a sense of "perceiving yourself perceiving" (Bishop 2012: 57).

Many installation artists believe in the ethics of their practice to collapse the distance that some scholars like Michael Fried have maintained as necessary. Where Fried insisted that distance was necessary for art to produce absorption, installation art aims to immerse spectators in a complete phenomenological experience; Fried articulates how absorption was a reaction against the superficial Rococo aesthetic of pop and how that manner of seeing became embedded in this early defining moment of art criticism. Art's cultural capital, in criticism and then history and theory, advances thereafter by "turning away from the exquisite, sensuous, intimately decorative painting that had held the field for roughly thirty years; and an insistence on the need to return to what were perceived as the high seriousness, elevated morality, and timeless esthetic principles of the great art of the past" (Fried 1988: 35). Bishop finds that Robert Irwin "considered the viewer's heightened consciousness and inclusion in the work to represent an ethical position" and quotes him as saying "by your individual participation in these situations, you may ... structure for yourself a 'new state of real', but it is you that does it, not me, and the individual responsibility to reason your own world view is the root implication" (Bishop 2012: 57). What you deem to constitute valuable in such an experience reveals an ethical value system. Quiet and dark are palpable in Hentschlagger's *No Exit Oasis* —made explicit for me because of their rarity across my life. A meditative quality descended that was also uncomfortable, similar to the awkwardness described by first time meditation students.

The various magnified objects in the space did not serve the purpose of cultivating close reflection, as those in Gannis' space had. Hentschlagger's objects seemed designed to define the dimensionality of the space and perhaps help participants orient themselves as they drifted half-aware around the space. The subdued atmosphere discourages rushing; even when wanting to get to some other part of the space, attempts at speed seemed a willful rejection of the spirit of the work. Since visiting *No Exit Oasis*, the tendency to scurry between online tabs and browsers has become more obvious. My city windows introduce light even at night, but so does the glow of various digital objects in my darkened home. There is a frenetic persistence to our connectivity these days, that I had intellectually recognized before arriving in Hentschlagger's work but whose work made more acutely palpable.

Producing artificial darkness is part of the effect in much of Hentschlagger's work, who speaks about the loss of darkness in the natural world and the impact on us and animals (Hentschlagger 2021). Dark rooms are patented in 1839 in England but these rooms don't offer visual darkness but chemical darkness, according to Noam F. Elcott, contributing to the establishment of artificial darkness (Elcott 2015: 0:35–31:46). Photography was predicated on darkness (an early name was schotography, the writing of shadows), but even that darkness fades away with the rise of electricity and the digital age. This is equally true in cinema. *No Exit Oasis* continues Hentschlagger's interest in producing dark spaces with controlled lighting elements. The closure of his own exhibitions and recognition that quarantines made in-person events difficult to plan led him to VR.

The title is a wry reference to the famed play by Sartre where people are trapped in a room and cannot escape each other for all eternity. The inability to exit was certainly an experience that some felt amidst the regulatory impositions that forced families and roommates to co-habitate without reprieve. On the other hand, he introduces the word oasis and the environment offers the potential for space from the incessant presence of the people in one's life. In quarantine, the desire to see friends and family was matched by a desperation to be free of them. The contradictions of this situation nicely situates the paradoxical infrastructure of creating a dark space by using a light-based medium like VR.

Hentschlagger expresses awareness that his work conditions response but also emphasizes that audiences' backgrounds and embededness in digital culture are likewise influential. My experience of being in Hentschalgger's work was dependent upon it, creating an interdependence that produces a decentered subject (Bishop 2012: 54). I am produced through engagement with a technological environment, perhaps obviously in the case of an immersive experience, but that merely highlights how the same occurs in browsing webpages, scanning social media posts, or swiping through dating apps. These highly corporatized environments invite a phenomenological context too, with psycho-social impact, but their content is so emphatic these more affective consequences of their websites and apps are frequently ignored. Likewise, the technological is made meaningful by my involvement and so is not asocial after all. In this convergence therefore we observe the necessity of the addressing these environments as extensions of our tangible world and evaluating how these spaces invade the tangible world to reshape it.

Performing the Metaverse

Gannis and Hentschlagger cultivate a contemplative mode on the world and self, but in the virtual environment, a different set of group behaviors and the etiquette has not yet been determined and socialized. After experiencing Matthew Gantt's performance *Welcome to the Doll's House* (2020) in Claudia Hart's virtual space *A Doll's House* (2020), we exchanged emails about the lack of clear social guidelines for navigating these spaces. This becomes even more important during this period where metaverse spaces proliferate. Gantt asked about the "questions of translating social norms from existing rituals, versus defining new ones in new spaces. Wonder how to show rather than tell?"[6] The showing rather than telling is a part of the social politics at stake in activating audiences within some installation art. Rather than creating additional authorities that inform and explain participatory politics, these projects invite audiences to determine what works for themselves (Fig. 7 & 8).

Fig. 7: Claudia Hart, A Doll's House XR, 2015/2020, web-based virtual reality on Mozilla Hubs

---

6   Email from Matthew Gantt, December 12, 2020.

Fig. 8: Claudia Hart, A Doll's House XR, 2015/2020, web-based virtual reality on Mozilla Hubs. performance-lecture in candy-corn avatar

For Gantt's four performances on December 4 and 10 to 13, 2020, audiences were encouraged to move around the space, to fly and roam at will. These instructions prior to the event's start encouraged a kind of exploratory sociality, with Hart modeling it by zooming about the space as Gantt performed. Gantt appeared as a whirling dervish styled avatar in the space, moving along to the sound scape he created in response to the Hentschlagger composition that is associated with the space. I discovered that I could move through walls, but also floors and found myself in the basement at one point because I wondered if anything would ever make me stop. Hart turns off the collisions with objects so that you glide through the structural components and appear suddenly in another space, beginning to observe the real parallels between the sonic and spatial simulacra. In the basement, Gantt's soundscape was muffled, but still present. Even though I was screen based, the audio made distance feel real— a reminder how important other senses are even within such a seemingly ocular-centric environment (Fig. 9).

Attending Gantt's performance in the space was the closest experience to the espoused value of a metaverse that would bring people together virtually, but his encouragement to explore our own potential in the space made it possible to push through the initial confusion on how to behave. Moving through walls became a literal and figurative opportunity to rethink what sociality means in a virtual environment where boundaries are selected and not imposed by laws like gravity. When choice is pervasive, or limited by design, other social politics arise. Hart's engagement with mixed reality performance has been described as creating "set pieces of reverie and reflection," which points to the theatrical that she invokes in relation to her work in mixed reality, but also the interest in placing audiences into strange situations (Hart n.d.). This is the work that theater has always done, but was energized by movements like Fluxus and Augusto Boal's community engagements that he unpacked in *Theater of the Oppressed* (1993). Many new media artists have turned to these practices to excite the potential of web connectivity as Noah Wardrip-Fruin and Nick Montfort make evident by including an excerpt in their *New Media Reader* (2003).

Fig. 9: Claudia Hart, A Doll's House XR, 2015/2020, web-based virtual reality on Mozilla Hubs, with Matthew Gantt performing live music in custom Hart avatar, directed by Claudia Hart and part of the Maker 2020 festival, Rome, curated by Hyphen-Hub.,

Hart and Gantt emphasize that using a digital space as a proscenium stage is boring. Keeping attendees active and moving is crucial, because it allows them the discovery process inherent to the social activation of installation art and its politics of social critique. Another project by Hart, *A Machiavelli Room*, was the stage for a set of readings directed by Asher Remy-Toledo titled *Ludicy*, on March 20 and 21, 2021. Those speakers who had audiences participate by showing them how to use the controls and indicating or encouraging these various functionalities within the context of their talk had greater response in the Q&A. Most audience members were new to social VR. Just as in *A Doll's House*, discovering how to be present while someone else is doing something requires trial and effort. The Hart sets are relatively static, which is why they compel performances, but simply being in them with a small group and learning how to move and converse produces unexpected social confusion. What does it mean to move through the body of another person's avatar? Does it matter if multiple conversations are happening at once? Why does someone need to "face" the performer or speaker? Does it matter if my avatar hovers in the space even when I am not present at the keyboard (Fig. 10)?

Fig. 10: Claudia Hart, Machiavelli World, 1994/2021, web-based virtual reality on Mozilla Hubs, including Hubs software interface and book, A Child's Machiavelli, 1994/2019.

Learning about this sociality is awkward for art audiences that typically want to feel knowledgeable, as Hart noticed about different groups (Hart 2021). People with backgrounds in theater had fewer issues being uncertain about an unfamiliar space, cloaked in costumes and designs (as an avatar), conversing across multiple languages (audio speech, chat text, and emoji). The cartooniness of the space makes palpable the way participants are both present and altered. The drive to authenticity in the visual arts is different in the performing arts where the actor is always straddling the various roles of day to day and performing life. We are all performing, intentionally or not (Butler 1988; Goffman 1990).

Hart talks about the spaces as sets wherein people can discover this new way of being. The theatrical language makes sense, but it also minimizes the intensity of the very real confusion about being both there and not there, embodied and disembodied, on screen and off. Though our data double of online life has been much theorized, we are still very much learning what it means to exist in person and online. There are some life experiences that many people describe as becoming real only once posted online, like the death of a beloved pet. Yet, many insist virtual spaces are not as real or meaningful. As a social species, we are still grappling with the various personas we present from work to home to bar to park, to which we must now add an assortment of online activities.

The purpose of writing about the works of Carla Gannis, Kurt Hentshlagger, Claudia Hart and Matthew Gantt using social virtual reality platforms as digital installations is to shift the emphasis from the material construct of the technology to one about content and experience. Discussing them as social VR or Mozilla Hubs projects diverts their intent for their means. This is not to deny the relevance of the formal structures that produce these spaces, but the software and hardware isn't the *only* thing relevant to appreciating or understanding these works. The realm of art's engagement with technology has been frequently sidelined in the narrative arcs of traditional art history. Alternatively, the technology has been minimized and misrepresented. For that reason, many computer arts scholars have stressed them in order to illuminate how they operate. To the degree that computer or digital art has developed its own story, that has occurred by emphasizing its application and use of assorted technologies. That is certainly apt, as is recognizing how such works relate to, expand upon, and reorient an extant discourse.

There is a kind of insistent novelty marketed alongside technologies that may enable capitalism but can undermine the ability to appreciate thoughtful works of art. What is new to many individuals as well as the larger social context is hybridity. The awareness of being both in a tangible world and the virtual at the same time is more pervasive. This is true when someone is scrolling social media or using augmented reality filters but VR emphasizes it in the way that it seems to negate the physical body's context. Similarly, installation art immerses audiences in an alternate reality even as audiences known it is 'just art.' But, operating from that liminal space allows people to struggle with the demands of these sometimes conflicting environments. Liminality used to be the provenance of tricksters, fools, and people transitioning from one stage of life to another (Hyde). Now, we are all forced to stand in that space of uncertainty.

Recognizing the framework that installation art has offered for fifty or more years can help us engage thoughtfully and creatively amidst the stark changes produced by the COVID pandemic as well as the slew of new technologies and online experiences being marshaled as improving upon base reality. These sites and products offer a spectacle that intentionally limits audiences' opportunity to consider the impact on them. This moment of confusion in shifting between the tangible and virtual can be usefully illuminated in the awareness cultivated by digital installations. Though there may be material differences in the instantiations of digital installations and those erected in the tangible realm, there are similarities in the social and political implications of engaging the psychological and phenomenological impact of these spaces. Given our hybridity, we need occasions that reflect on that without the occasion becoming branded by a commercial entity, as will occur all too soon.

References

Bell, Genevieve. 2022. 'The metaverse is just a new word for an old idea'. *MIT Technology Review*. February 8 2022. https://www.technologyreview.com/2022/02/08/1044732/metaverse-history-snow-crash/

Bishop, Claire. 2012. *Installation Art: A Critical History*. Reprinting of the ed. 2005. London: Tate Publ.

Blum, Michael. 2017. 'A More Accessible and Eclectic Future for Virtual Reality'. *Hyperallergic*. March 7, 2017. https://hyperallergic.com/363836/a-more-accessible-and-eclectic-future-for-virtual-reality/

Bogard, Paul. 2014. *The End of Night: Searching for Natural Darkness in an Age of Artificial Light*.

Butler, Judith. 1988. 'Performative Acts and Gender Constitution: An Essay in Phenomenology and Feminist Theory'. *Theatre Journal* 40 (4): 519–31. https://doi.org/10.2307/3207893.

'Cabinets of Curiosity: The Web as Wunderkammer—The Appendix'. n.d. Accessed 6 March 2022. https://theappendix.net/posts/2012/11/cabinets-of-curiosity-the-web-as-wunderkammer.

Carpo, Mario. 2017. 'space Odyssey: The Rise of 3D Technology'. *Art Forum* 55 (7).

Clark, T. J. 2006. *The Sight of Death: An Experiment in Art Writing*. New Haven: Yale University Press.

Crary, Jonathan. 2014. *24/7: Late Capitalism and the Ends of Sleep*. London: Verso.

Denson, G. Roger. 2017. 'The Splendid Phenomenology of Hentschlägerian Voids'. In *Splendid Voids: The Immersive Works of Kurt Hentschläger: SOL-Installation 2017, ZEE-Installation 2008, FEED-Performance 2005*, edited by Isabelle Meiffert. Berlin: Distanz.

Elcott, Noam Milgrom. *Noam M. Elcott: Artificial Darkness*. SONIC ACTS Festival - The Geologic Imagination. 27 February 2015 - Paradiso, Amsterdam, the Netherlands. https://www.youtube.com/watch?v=uodf2eS4tkc&t=1835s

—. 2018. *Artificial Darkness: An Obscure History of Modern Art and Media*. University of Chicago Press.

Engberg, Maria, and Jay David Bolter. 2020. "The aesthetics of reality media'. Journal of Visual Culture 19 (1): 81–95.

Fernandez, Judith Amores, Anna Fusté, Robert Richer, and Pattie Maes. 2019. 'Deep Reality: An Underwater VR Experience to Promote Relaxation by Unconscious HR, EDA, and Brain Activity Biofeedback'. In *ACM SIGGRAPH 2019 Virtual, Augmented, and Mixed Reality*, 1. SIGGRAPH '19. New York, NY, USA: Association for Computing Machinery. https://doi.org/10.1145/3306449.3328818.

Findlay, Michael. 2012. *The Value of Art*. Pretel Verlag.

Fried, Michael. 1988. *Absorption and Theatricality: Painting and Beholder in the Age of Diderot*. Chicago: University of Chicago Press.

Gannis, Carla. 2021. https://vimeo.com/541329940

Goffman, Erving. 1990. *The Presentation of Self in Everyday Life*. New York: Anchor Books.
Graham, Brian, Gregory John Ashworth, and John E. Tunbridge. 2005. 'The Uses and Abuses of Heritage'. In *Heritage, Museums and Galleries: An Introductory Reader*, edited by Gerard Corsane. New York: Routledge.
Grau, Oliver. 2003. *Virtual Art: From Illusion to Immersion*. Cambridge, Mass.: MIT Press.
Greengard, Samuel. 2019. *Virtual Reality*. Cambridge: MIT Press.
Hart, Claudia. 2021. Artist Talk: Hyphen Hub New York City. June 16. 7–9pm.
—. n.d. 'Mixed Reality Worlds'. Tumblr. Accessed 18 June 2021a. https://claudiahart-mixedreality.tumblr.com/.
—. n.d. 'The Dolls'. ClaudiaHart.Com. Accessed 18 June 2021b. https://claudiahart.com/The-Dolls.
Hentschlager, Kurt. n.d. 'Bio'. Kurt Hentschlager. Accessed 18 June 2021. http://www.kurthentschlager.com/bio.html.
—. 2021. Artist Talk: Hyphen Hub New York City. June 16. 7–9pm.
Hillis, Ken. 1999. *Digital Sensations: Space, Identity, and Embodiment in Virtual Reality*. Minneapolis: University of Minnesota Press.
Hyde, Lewis. 2020. *Trickster Makes this World: Mischief, Myth, and Art*. New York: Farrar, Strauss & Giroux.
Kelly, Michael. 2008. *Oxford Encyclopedia of Aesthetics*. Oxford University Press.
Kent, Charlotte. 2022. 'Beyond Representation in Virtual Reality: The Abstract Art of Jane Hamill and Kevin Mack'. *Leonardo*, August, 1–10. https://doi.org/10.1162/leon_a_02139.
Koeppe, Wolfram. 2002. 'Collecting for the Kunstkammer'. The Met's Heilbrunn Timeline of Art History. October 2002. https://www.metmuseum.org/toah/hd/kuns/hd_kuns.htm.
Krauss, Rosalind. 1979. 'sculpture in the Expanded Field'. *October* 8: 31–44. https://doi.org/10.2307/778224.
Lanier, Jaron. 2017. *Dawn of the New Everything: Encounters with Reality and Virtual Reality*. New York: Henry Holt and Company.
Pelizza, Analisa. 2018. *Communities at a Crossroads: Material Semiotics for Online Sociability in the Fade of Cyberculture*. Amsterdam: Institute of Network Cultures. https://networkcultures.org/blog/publication/tod-28-communities-at-a-crossroads/.
Polansky, Lana. 2021. 'Part III: The Fuzzy Science and Art of Empathy'. *Rhizome*. 24 March 2021. http://rhizome.org/editorial/2021/mar/24/part-iii-the-fuzzy-science-and-art-of-empathy/.
Riva, Giuseppe, Fabrizia Mantovani, and Brenda K. Wiederhold. 2020. 'Positive Technology and COVID-19'. *Cyberpsychology, Behavior, and Social Networking* 23 (9): 581–87. https://doi.org/10.1089/cyber.2020.29194.gri.

Rizzo, Albert "Skip", and Sebastian Thomas Koenig. 2017. 'Is Clinical Virtual Reality Ready for Primetime?' *Neuropsychology* 31 (8): 877–99. https://doi.org/10.1037/neu0000405.

Schor, Mira. 1996. 'Patrilineage (1991–92).' In *Wet: On Painting, Feminism, and Art Culture*, 98–118. Duke University Press. https://doi.org/10.2307/j.ctv12100vp.

Smith, Matthew Wilson. 2007. *The Total Work of Art: From Bayreuth to Cyberspace*. New York: Routledge.

The Art Newspaper. 2022. 'What is the metaverse and why does it matter to the art world? Experts weigh in and predict its future impact'. January 28 2022. https://www.theartnewspaper.com/2022/01/28/what-is-the-metaverse-and-why-does-it-matter-to-the-art-world-experts-weigh-in-and-predict-its-future-impact

United Nations. About – UN Virtual Reality. http://unvr.sdgactioncampaign.org/home/about/#.YrBts5DMJfU

Biographical Notes

Giota Alevizou is a lecturer in Humanistic Computing at the Department of Digital Humanities at King's College London (KCL). She has expertise on the historical and political economic aspects of digital transformation, particularly on the ways in which data literacies, ethics and citizenship intersect with information politics, knowledge, and education cultures. She has published widely on cultural politics of digital & knowledge media, collective intelligence and civic technologies.

Christopher Frieß studies TransArts at the University of Applied Arts Vienna. He has been the recipient of several grants and competitions (2022 CAPE 10 Art Contest Winner; 2019 Merit Scholarship | University of Applied Arts Vienna). His recent exhibitions include *Perceive* in Innsbruck main station; *Thread Lightly When Close to the Railway* in L'Almacén of Geneva, and *A shop is a shop is a shop* in Kunsthalle Vienna.

Charlotte Kent is an arts writer and assistant professor of visual culture at Montclair State University, with a particular interest in digital culture and the absurd. She is co-editor with Katherine Guinness of *Contemporary Absurdities, Existential Crises, and Visual Art* (forthcoming, Intellect Books). She is an Editor-at-Large with a monthly columnist on Art & Technology for *The Brooklyn Rail* and writes for various magazines and academic journals, occasionally contributing essays to catalogues and books.

Felix Maschewski is the co-director of the Critical Data Lab at Humboldt University and a teaching fellow at the University of Basel. His book *The Society of Wearables* (written with Anna-Verena Nosthoff) was published by Nicolai Publishing and Intelligence in 2019. In addition to academic publications, he writes regularly for *Frankfurter Allgemeine Zeitung, Zeit Online, Neue Zürcher Zeitung, Wirtschaftswoche, Jacobin, Philosophie Magazin, Die Republik, Der Tagesspiegel, Hohe Luft* and *tazFuturZwei* (column), among others.

Eve Murchison has recently graduated from King's College London MA in Digital Culture and Society with Distinction. Her research has explored the role of digital technologies in relation to health, biopower and biopolitics. Currently an NHS employee, she plans to pursue a doctorate in the field of bioethics and digital health.

Anna-Verena Nosthoff is the co-director of the Critical Data Lab at Humboldt University and a visiting researcher at Princeton University. From spring 2023, she will also be a visiting fellow at the LSE (Media Department). Recently, she has holded visiting, research and teaching positions at the University of Vienna, FU Berlin, and at Weizenbaum Institut/ WZB.

Julia Ramírez-Blanco is senior researcher (Ramón y Cajal Program) in the Art History Department of Madrid´s Complutense University. Her interdisciplinary work connects art history, visual culture, utopian studies, and activist movements. Her latest publications include the books *Artistic Utopias of Revolt* (Palgrave, 2018), *15M. El tiempo de las plazas* [M15. The Time of the *Plazas*] (Alianza, 2021), and *Amigos, disfraces y comunas* [Friends, Costumes and Communes] (Cátedra, 2022).

Ramón Reichert works as a senior researcher and teaches and researches at the University of Applied Arts Vienna, Department of Cultural Studies. He is Senior lecturer for Philosophy of Science and Methods of Social Research, Baden-Württemberg, Cooperative State University Mosbach, Germany. His current research project is "Visual politics and protest. Artistic research project on the visual framing of the Russia-Ukraine war on internet portals and social media" (2022–23). His latest book publication is *Selfies: Self-thematization in Digital Image Culture* (2023).

Francesco Spampinato is an Associate Professor in the Department of the Arts at the University of Bologna. His research in contemporary art history and visual studies focuses on the relationships between contemporary art, media, and technology. His latest publications include the book *Art vs. TV: A Brief History of Contemporary Artists' Responses to Television* (Bloomsbury Academic, 2022). Spampinato is also co-editor with Julia Ramírez-Blanco of the anthology *The Pandemic Visual Regime: Visuality and Performativity in the COVID-19 Crisis* (Punctum Books, 2023).

Christina Tente is a PhD candidate at the Department of Cultural Sciences at the University of Gothenburg, Sweden. Her research focuses on memes, media, non-human photography, and the visual culture of the COVID-19 pandemic. Her research interests include media studies, posthuman theory, dance research, digital (im)materialities, and non-conforming bodies. She has collaborated with cultural organizations in Greece and Sweden.